Praise for Cloud Data Warehousing

"Barry Devlin has taken on the task of examining how the cloud changes data warehousing. No, it's not just about being "cloud native." Barry outlines what's different, why it matters, and what to do about it. A must read." — Merv Adrian, Founder and Principal, IT Market Strategy

"Once again, Barry Devlin has sharpened the focus on new trends in data architecture, explaining what's new, what's not, and what matters. For more than 30 years, Barry has placed enterprise data architectures on a firm footing with his insights and frameworks. For data veterans and newbies alike, this new volume will edify, instruct, and keep readers on the right path." — Wayne Eckerson, President, Eckerson Group

"The cloud database and analytics industry is evolving rapidly, with new approaches and radical enhancements. As one of the original thinkers in data warehousing, Barry Devlin's forty years of experience and knowledge of current thinking brings welcome perspective. He explains trends and navigates the landscape in a clear, practical manner, to help design, implement, and benefit from emerging systems. As always, his writing is thought provoking and enjoyable, and will be of interest to anyone working in this area." — Henry Cook, Gartner

"In 1988, Devlin and Murphy published a vision of analytic architecture. Millions of jobs and billions of dollars later, we're almost finished building it. Barry Devlin's new cloud books are the design pattern for the next era." — Dan Graham, PM director for IBM SP2 and Teradata 6700.

Cloud Data Warehousing

Volume I: Architecting Data Warehouse, Lakehouse, Mesh, and Fabric

Dr. Barry Devlin

Technics Publications

Published by:

115 Linda Vista, Sedona, Arizona USA
https://www.TechnicsPub.com

Edited by Jamie Hoberman
Cover design by Lorena Molinari

First Printing 2023
Copyright © 2023 by Barry Devlin

ISBN, print ed.	9781634623360
ISBN, Kindle ed.	9781634623377
ISBN, ePub ed.	9781634623384
ISBN, PDF ed.	9781634623407

Library of Congress Control Number: 2023938546

To Dear Friends, Colleagues, and Clients
over Four Decades of Data Warehousing

Without you, this book would
never have been written

My special thanks go to my good friends, Dan Graham, Thomas Frisendal, and Dave Wells, who reviewed the first draft. Your input has improved the book immeasurably.

Gratitude also to my publisher, Steve Hoberman, who did so much to get this book quickly and elegantly to press, and to Lorena Molinari for her stunning cover art.

CONTENTS

Chapter 1: Cloud Data Warehousing: What and Why? _____ 1

In the beginning was data warehousing _____ 3

The book _____ 5

Takeaways _____ 8

Chapter 2: Data Warehousing: A Short History _____ 11

Enter the data warehouse _____ 13

From logical data warehouse to data fabric _____ 25

By the data lake we find a lakehouse _____ 31

Catching the data mess in a data mesh _____ 43

Data warehousing today—In one picture _____ 48

Takeaways _____ 52

Chapter 3: Data Warehousing—Purpose and Principles _____ 55

The Purpose of Cloud Data Warehousing _____ 56

One last time: data vs. information _____ 57

Seven deadly sins of data warehousing _____ 63

Five foundational principles of cloud data warehousing _____ 68

Three thinking spaces for cloud data warehousing _____ 74

Takeaways _____ 89

Chapter 4: Cloud Data Warehousing Logical Architecture __91

Information domains and types _____ 93

The tri-domain+ information model _____ 94

Introducing information pillars _____ 104

Fleshing out the function _____ 115

Takeaways _____ 133

Chapter 5: Blue Skies and Cloud Architecture _____ 135

It's the AI, stupid _____ 136

Technology-driven evolution _____ 142

Takeaways _____ 156

Chapter 6: The Journey to Cloud Data Warehousing _____ 159

Now, architectural design patterns _____ 161

Starting point: Existing on-premises DWC _____ 167

Migration from the DWC _____ 168

Starting point: Existing on-premises or cloud DLC _____ 174

Migration from the DLC _____ 176

Starting Point: Ongoing cloud uptake _____ 180

Takeaways _____ 186

Chapter 7: And that's a Wrap _____ 189

References _____ 199

Index _____ 207

Chapter 1

Cloud Data Warehousing: What and Why?

> *Rows and flows of angel hair*
> *And ice cream castles in the air*
> *And feather canyons everywhere*
> *I've looked at clouds that way.*
>
> *Both Sides Now*, Joni Mitchell

Cloud data warehousing is now a reality, neither castle in the air, feathered canyon, nor angel hair. It has become a highly desired and desirable goal in the world of IT and data management. Except that its meaning is just slightly—well—cloudy. In fact, it is darkly obscure to many.

Over the past few years, a stream of consultants, experts, and vendors have attempted to craft the perfect solution to "cloud data warehousing." So, we've had quite a few cloud data warehouses. A data lakehouse. Not to mention data fabric and data mesh. Perhaps more to come.

What could possibly go wrong?

Quite a lot, I would suggest. Especially the extensive confusion likely caused among those enterprises and engineers trying to migrate an existing data warehouse or lake to the cloud or, less common, those trying to implement cloud data warehousing from scratch.

My goal in this book and its sequel is to help those trying to understand and implement cloud data warehousing. Its audience is the managers and architects—perhaps new to data warehousing—who make the high-level decisions about their enterprise's overall approach. It is not a deep technical dive into the minutiae of instances, regions, or cloud-specific performance or pricing. The aim is to help designers avoid the many pitfalls inherent in a situation where multiple overlapping and often contradictory definitions and terminology are being offered by the proponents of each approach.

Volume I sets out to clearly explain what cloud data warehousing is—from first principles. The meaning of data and information; and how to deliver and manage them irrespective of their location on-premises or in the cloud. To describe how to architect and design an environment that supports insight-inspired decision making and action taking. To propose a common *lingua franca* to discuss and debate the emerging terminology of lakehouses, fabrics, and meshes. And to offer guidance for the first, tentative steps on a journey to implementation.

Volume II dives deeper into the various flavors—cloud data warehouse, data lakehouse, data fabric, and data mesh—that have occupied the attention of vendors and implementers over the past few years. It offers an independent view and assessment of what each means and promises. It explores the pros and cons of each. And compares them to one another, with a view to suggesting in which circumstances you might choose one over the other.

But let's start at the beginning. (A very good place to start.)

IN THE BEGINNING WAS DATA WAREHOUSING

Data warehousing is a concept rapidly approaching its fortieth birthday. Over the decades, it has been conflated with business intelligence (BI) and analytics. It has been confused with data lakes and big data. The term has been both deified and denigrated. But it has survived. Longer than many complementing or competing terms.

Throughout this book and its companion, I use the phrase *data warehousing* to encompass all of the many methods and models that have emerged since the mid-1980s. Their purpose: to describe how data—or, more correctly, information—can be put to work to help decision makers of all levels—from factory floor operatives to data scientists to CEOs—to understand what is happening in the business and the world in which it operates, why it is happening, and what to do about it, now and in the future.

From humble reports, through queries and spreadsheets, dashboards, and BI suites, to data mining and analytics, and further to algorithms, artificial intelligence (AI), and decision intelligence, I place all these topics within the remit of this simple, perhaps old-fashioned phrase. Why? Because each and every one of these means of delivering insights to the business depends on getting the underlying data right. That was and is the first and fundamental purpose of data warehousing: *the delivery of consistent, integrated, timely, quality, useful, and usable data primarily to business users.*

Not unexpectedly, I use the phrase *cloud data warehousing* to mean exactly the same delivery services as above, but in the cloud, as well as hybrid and multi-cloud.

The challenge with this data delivery goal has long been that it bores the business. It's just plumbing. Visual BI tools depicting profit and loss in bright colors are more interesting. AI and its promises are exciting to businesspeople because they just want results, preferably with minimal effort. These business-facing tools are the golden taps from which insights and right action flow. Now, *that* gets the attention of the business. But, the data plumbing— let's leave that to IT.

Now the plumbing is undergoing perhaps the biggest transformation seen in all the history of data warehousing: the move to the cloud. To be clear, the cloud does *not* change the purpose or principles of data warehousing. In some respects, cloud increases their importance. As we shall see later, cloud does not, in most cases, even test the fundamental, generalized architecture of data warehousing.

However, beyond its many promises and benefits, the cloud has certainly caused many people to question the thinking, methods, and tools used in traditional data warehousing. All of which has led to an entire crop of divergent approaches to implementing cloud data warehousing, as mentioned above. And with such a diverse menu of terminology, techniques, and tooling comes a real dilemma of choice.

THE BOOK

We start with a review of the history of data warehousing, exploring the breadth of thinking included in the concept and noting its varied and often conflicting terminology. Together, these factors explain the longevity of data warehousing—how many times has it been declared dead and arisen from its ashes?—but also the many ways in which implementation has gone astray.

Next up is a chapter on the purpose and principles of data warehousing, seen through the lens of multiple decades of experience. It is vital that the purpose and principles are understood when considering a migration to the cloud or, indeed, any major reworking or expansion of the technological foundation of an existing implementation. Too often, vendors and implementers emphasize the novelty and benefits of new infrastructure without addressing their relevance either to the underpinning rationale for data warehousing or to its real implementation challenges. This discussion of purpose and principles leads to a conceptual architecture for data warehousing. It turns out that this conceptual level of architecture remains exactly the same, whether implementation is planned on-premises or in the cloud.

Chapter four provides an overview of a comprehensive logical architecture for all forms of cloud data warehousing. Both this and the prior conceptual level can together be called the Digital Information Systems Architecture (DISA). This is based first on the thinking in *Business unIntelligence* (Devlin, 2013) and subsequently expanded over the intervening decade.

We note that this level of architecture is largely agnostic to the question of where the solution is delivered, whether on-premises, cloud, or hybrid. The chapter, therefore, describes the original logical architecture and then explores where cloud data warehousing requires a change in perspective.

We turn our eyes to the future in chapter five. First up are the ethical and societal challenges of artificial intelligence and how they must be addressed in cloud data warehousing. That is followed by a deeper dive into some considerations of data storage and databases as technology evolves, as well as how the demanding topic of context and the meaning of data will need to be addressed.

Finally, we examine how existing, traditional data warehousing solutions and current cloud-based systems can be migrated to cloud data warehousing, hopefully without necessitating a complete reworking of everything that has been previously, successfully achieved. Rather than attempting this with theoretical purity—which is, in any case, impossible—we explore it from the perspective of three different, practical starting points and a set of architectural design patterns that emerge from them. Most implementers of cloud data warehousing will start from some mix of these starting points and patterns, but the lessons will be equally applicable to all, irrespective of the journey they are undertaking.

Volume II, Implementing Data Warehouse, Lakehouse, Mesh, and Fabric, as the name implies, dives deeper into all these topics and more, with the explicit aim of comparing the strengths and weaknesses of these emerging patterns of cloud data warehousing.

TAKEAWAYS

- *Data warehousing,* as used here, encompasses all the many approaches that have emerged in the market since the mid-1980s to provide data and information to decision makers of all levels. Its purpose is to help them understand what is happening in the business (and the world in which it operates), why, and what to do about it, now and in the future.

- The fundamental driver of data warehousing is the delivery of consistent, integrated, timely, quality, useful, and usable data. Absent a balanced set of these qualities, data is literally garbage. Insights are far from insightful. And decisions are dubious at best.

- Although data warehousing technology is undergoing arguably the biggest transformation—the move to the cloud—that has been seen in all its history, adhering to the drivers and principles of data warehousing remains as important as ever.

- And as if migration to cloud data warehousing isn't challenging enough for stretched and stressed IT staff, a plethora of new terms—data lakehouse, data fabric, and data mesh—has emerged. Each has its own intellectual baggage, as well as unique strengths and weaknesses, all of which must be understood and evaluated as part of the move.

- The goal of this book and Volume II, therefore, is to explore and explain at a high level the true meaning of cloud data warehousing. Building on four decades of successful implementations (and not forgetting failures), a variety of architectural approaches to delivering data and information to decision makers is discussed. All of which provide a sound basis for comparing the diverse solutions now being proposed in the market and deciding which one (or combination) of them best suits your future needs.

Chapter 2

DATA WAREHOUSING: A SHORT HISTORY

*You can't really know where you are going
until you know where you have been.*

Maya Angelou

In 1988, a cell phone weighed roughly two pounds, cost $4,000, offered thirty minutes of talk time—and no other function—having taken ten hours to charge. The Motorola DynaTAC 8000X was fondly known as "the brick" and was wildly popular ear-candy among the jet set of the time[1].

The same year, your office desk might have been adorned with an Apple Macintosh II or an IBM PS/2 with 512K of memory, a 20MB hard drive—if you were lucky—and a

---

[1] Parts of this chapter were first published by and are reprinted with permission of 1105 Media, Inc. (Devlin, 2018).

choice of a monochrome or color monitor with an eye-catching resolution of 640x480 pixels.

Of more interest for data warehousing would have been the Teradata DBC/1012, a massively parallel processing database system with a thousand processors and five terabytes of disk storage at the very top of the range. Few customers reached those dizzying heights: the costs were eye-watering. Although Teradata is now almost synonymous with data warehousing, its marketing material spoke only of a "Data Base Computer System", because the phrase *data warehouse* had only just been unleashed on an unsuspecting world.

ON THE MEANINGS OF WORDS

As any practitioner knows, a plethora of definitions and pseudo-definitions exist for the terms *data warehouse*, *data mart*, *data lake*, and all the others used in this section. In this history, we'll use all these terms lightly and with loose definitions. It's the work of the next two chapters to define them more precisely.

Together with *data warehousing*, whose specific usage in these books was defined earlier, I use two other terms with specific meanings throughout. **Decision-making support** is used to cover traditional reporting, querying, BI, and dash-boarding in support of businesspeople making decisions based on historical data. **Analytics** covers data mining, statistical analysis, extending to the use of machine learning (ML) and AI to explore data, predict future outcomes, and automatically prescribe actions. Gartner has coined the acronym, ABI (Analytics and Business Intelligence), to cover both these areas together, as the boundary between them becomes increasingly blurred.

ENTER THE DATA WAREHOUSE

In 1988, Paul Murphy and I published the first description of a data warehouse architecture in the IBM Systems Journal. Entitled "An architecture for a business and[2] information system" (Devlin and Murphy, 1988), the article summarized internal work in IBM leading to the "EMEA [Europe, Middle East, and Africa] Business Information System (EBIS) architecture as the strategic direction for informational systems [that proposes] an integrated warehouse of company data based firmly in the relational database environment."

The genesis of this work and, indeed data warehousing, dates to the mid-1960s, when businesspeople, particularly in finance functions, began to request extracts of data from mainframe operational systems for reporting and problem

---

[2] That extraneous "and" was inserted by an unknown editor and missed in proofreading by the authors (oops!).

solving. This led to the development of decision support systems (DSS) and executive information systems (EIS), such as Easytrieve and similar products (Power, 2009). The challenge that emerged in the 1980s was that IT found that a "rat's nest" of unmaintained and unmaintainable population programs had grown up that was delivering multiple, inconsistent copies of data to different departments. For IBM, EBIS was to be the solution to the ensuing management confusion.

The key architectural figure of the article, reproduced here in *Figure 2.1*, would be instantly recognizable by any modern data warehouse practitioner. Front and center is the **business data warehouse (BDW)**: a single logical repository containing public and personal data at raw, detailed, and summary levels from operational and local (personal) systems. *Raw* here meant *transactional*, rather than its more modern senses of *unprocessed* or *uncontextualized*.

This data is described in a **business data directory** sourced from a data dictionary and business process definitions. This was seen as a key support to the end-user interface that made data available to businesspeople via workstations and reports. It is the direct precursor of metadata storage in the modern data catalog and business glossary.

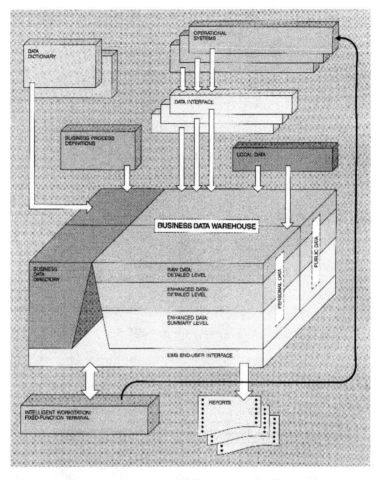

Figure 2.1: Overview of the EMEA Business Information System (Devlin and Murphy, 1988)

The structure of the data in the BDW is also illustrated in the article as a conceptual set of tables—such as customers, employees, products, orders, and so on—matching the users' perceptions of the structure and meaning of business information they access and use.

The data interface and interface to operational systems (not shown here) are responsible for populating the BDW from the operational systems. They are the clear precursors to the **extract, transform, and load (ETL)** tools that emerged a few years later and remain—under a variety of guises and names—central to all approaches to data warehousing.

Embedded here, but unmentioned, is the fundamental idea that operational and informational systems are separate from one another. We will return to this assumption in *"Seven deadly sins of data warehousing"*.

IBM rolled the concepts of this architecture into the IBM Information Warehouse Framework in 1991. Focused on a proprietary approach and, trademarking the term *Information Warehouse*, IBM missed the opportunity to define and monetize the data warehousing market. It turns out that trademark is, in retrospect, unfortunate. Information is surely more representative of what a warehouse should deliver, but we are left with the term *data warehouse* for general use, and it was this phrase that Bill Inmon popularized in the early 1990s (Inmon, 1992).

BUT... WHAT IS A DATA WAREHOUSE?

It was also Inmon who introduced the oft-quoted definition of a data warehouse: a subject-oriented, nonvolatile, integrated, time-variant collection of data in support of management decisions. The four data characteristics of this simple and memorable definition are implicit in the EBIS architecture and are emergent in Inmon's 1992 book. As the basis for much thinking about what a data warehouse looks like, these terms bear closer inspection.

- *Subject-oriented:* This corresponds to the idea that data should be represented in terms and structures, such as customer, product, order, transaction, etc., that are familiar to businesspeople. A more formal interpretation aligns the terms and structures to the **enterprise data model** described by John Zachman (Sowa and Zachman, 1992). Both map to the primary purpose of the data warehouse: The subject-oriented view is framed to directly support decision makers, while an enterprise data model is aimed more at integrating data from diverse sources to make it more useful and usable.

- *Nonvolatile:* In simple terms, this reflects a long-standing business need to be able to recreate a business situation as of a particular date and time in the past, either for reporting or as a basis for what-if simulations. Therefore, unlike many operational systems and modern external data sources, a data warehouse must maintain an ongoing and stable record of both current and historical data states. Ideally, also, data is never deleted.

- **_Integrated:_** This characteristic springs from the under-standing that data extracted from diverse operational sources may be incoherent for reasons of meaning (e.g., different definitions of "profit") or timing (due to time zones or other reasons). Integration means reconciling these differences in various ways to deliver a **single version of the truth (SVOT)** that can be used across the enterprise. SVOT has long since been recognized as an ideal that is unachievable in practice. However, integration of key data to common standards remains an important goal for data warehousing, although under-emphasized in both the data lake and data mesh.

- **_Time-variant:_** All data records in the warehouse are versioned to preserve data changes in the operational sources as far as possible. This is a consequence of the nonvolatile characteristic above and is achieved via timestamping of the records. However, the exact nature of the timestamp has long been debated. The simplest approach, as described by Inmon, is to record the time of (batch) loading into the warehouse. However, this method misses multiple updates between batch loads and, more generally, is insufficient for many business purposes. Therefore, bitemporal and, more recently tri-temporal, schemas—where each record carries multiple timestamps—have been implemented or promoted in the past decade to provide more and better ways of analyzing and using data over time (Johnston, 2014).

As experienced data warehouse practitioners are aware, these characteristics are neither complete nor fully congruent. At a high level, they provide welcome guidance for design. Nonetheless, every data warehouse implementation ends up balancing them against one another and trading them off against business needs and the limitations of chosen or required technology. One example of such a trade-off involves simplifying integration by focusing on a subject-oriented data warehouse for a single department, perhaps better called a data mart. Another example is the dimensional data warehouse, discussed in the following section, where business demands for early delivery are accommodated by redefining the concept of subject orientation.

This situation continues to this day. Despite claims to the contrary, data lakes do not eliminate the need for these compromises, and in some cases, promote practices contrary to the above characteristics, as well as introduce new challenges, as discussed in *"Diving into the data lake."*

COMPETING DATA WAREHOUSE STRUCTURES

What is missing from the EBIS architecture and, indeed, from Inmon's early book is the hub-and-spoke structure of a centralized **enterprise data warehouse (EDW)** that provides the reconciliation point for data from diverse sources feeding multiple departmental—or otherwise segmented—**data marts**. This structure, sometimes referred to as the *Inmon data warehouse*, arose first from technological necessity: General purpose relational databases (RDBs) in the 1990s weren't powerful enough to handle multiple concurrent user queries with varying data needs against a single, enterprise-level, subject-oriented database.

One solution—and the solution that sticks most closely to the intent and principles of the original architecture—was to split the data warehouse into two, or sometimes more, layers. As shown in *Figure 2.2*, data is integrated/reconciled in the EDW and then distributed to businesspeople in more query-friendly, departmentally focused data marts.

This approach comes with two major challenges. First, its layering implies that at least some part of the EDW—often found to be quite a large part—must be built before any data marts can be delivered. Business needs, therefore, are delayed, and a careful, program-based, project management approach is a prerequisite to balancing business demands with the challenging reality of data diversity. Second, data must be moved sequentially from layer to layer, so each additional layer delays the arrival of data to where it's needed.

With timeliness of decisions becoming increasingly important, such delays are unwelcome.

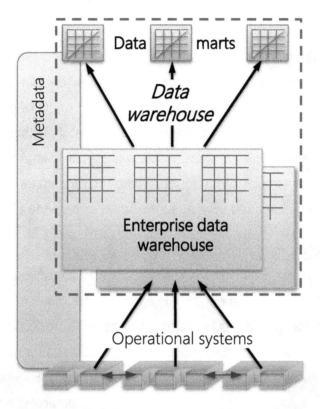

Figure 2.2: The layered data warehouse architecture (Devlin, 1997)

Dr. Ralph Kimball took a different approach to solving these build and runtime delays. He adopted a different data model and database structure optimized for the most common type of analysis: slice-and-dice and drill-down. This approach is the **dimensional** or **star-schema data warehouse** (Kimball, 1998). It starts from the immediate analysis needs of departmental business processes to create a performant database consisting only of relevant facts and dimensions. Departmental-level star schemas are subsequently related via conformed dimensions.

By the turn of the century, the debate between these two approaches had allegedly turned into a war (Breslin, 2004); whether concocted by the press or for the benefit of one or other of the parties remains unclear. The reality is that each approach has its strengths and weaknesses. In many cases, a hybrid approach can be taken, where the data marts are dimensional and fed from a reconciliation layer in the EDW.

Since the beginning of the new millennium, technological advances in both hardware and software have offered substantially improved performance in relational databases. The need for data marts and star schemas and the debate between them was thus reduced. This enabled some products to return to the concept described in the original EBIS architecture: logical relational views supporting the access needs of different user groups built on the same underlying physical database tables.

OPERATIONAL BI AND THE ODS

By the mid-1990s, businesspeople were becoming more demanding. The requirement for results from the last month or week morphed into a demand for yesterday's figures and, from there to something approaching real-time, often called operational BI. Such timeliness demands can stretch a layered architecture to its limits.

Various workarounds were proposed, of which the most common was the **operational data store (ODS[3])**, a new layer of (at best) semi-consolidated data, sourced almost continuously from the operational systems, and positioned between them and the EDW (Inmon, et al., 1996). Of course, the gains in timeliness were offset by the losses in consistency of the data provided to the business. As we shall see again and again, this trade-off between timeliness and consistency remains a conundrum even to this day.

SO, WHAT DOES THIS TELL US?

History is of value only in what we can learn from it. In its early days, the data warehouse—although limited in its business aims and restricted by the technology of the time—offers four important lessons that apply in varying degrees to all the types of data warehousing that have emerged since:

1. *Data meaning is central:* Data warehousing, despite its geeky name, exists for businesspeople to meet their decision-making needs. Therefore, data as traditionally stored in computer systems is insufficient. We need to

---

[3] It amuses me that ODS said quickly sounds like odious.

add context to make it meaningful. As described later, it needs to be transformed into information.

2. ***Data quality is key:*** Garbage in, garbage out. Yes, that old adage applies here—forcefully. Data must be cleansed before use by the business. Such cleansing spans from fixing tiny errors within the data to making sure that the data is consistent and integrated despite its multiple different and possibly misaligned sources. This is the main reason for centralizing the data in a warehouse and, in particular, in the EDW.

3. ***Data timeliness increasingly matters:*** The earliest users of the data warehouse were happy to get a correct total for last month's sales. Today, digital business demands sub-second responses, in many cases, to much more complex queries. In addition, multi-month development cycles have gone seriously out of fashion. The Kimball approach to warehousing was a direct response to the early needs for timeliness. As we shall see next, the data lake is similarly driven.

4. ***It's tough to balance the above three requirements:*** None of the above can be ignored. Nor can they be *simultaneously and fully* met in a single solution, although some of the more advanced and powerful databases may approach this ideal. Different tools and approaches

to data warehousing usually favor one over the others. In most cases, they need to be balanced and traded off against one another, a process requiring significant design skills in warehouse implementers.

As data warehousing migrates to the cloud, the trade-offs become more difficult. The cloud is highly distributed, spans time zones, and may span national borders. All these factors pose additional challenges to balancing these prime requirements of data meaning, quality, and timeliness.

We will see the same lessons repeatedly throughout the history of data warehousing. The data lake and data mesh approaches emphasize them strongly.

FROM LOGICAL DATA WAREHOUSE TO DATA FABRIC

The original EBIS architecture envisaged a "single logical storehouse of all information... [that] may physically reside in multiple locations." However, practical implementation was limited to a single physical database by the technological limitations of relational databases of the time. Since then, RDBs have delivered increasingly powerful federated function and support for virtual and materialized views that enable the original vision to be realized. The terms *federated* or *virtual data warehouse* are often used for such systems.

By the early 2000s, however, it was clear that copying all data into a data warehouse could not meet many types of decision-making needs. As customers went online and demanded instant responses, decision makers required direct and immediate access to multiple and varied source systems, in addition to the warehouse, to meet these demands.

Enterprise information integration and data virtualization software promised such access. An array of front-end tools connecting users and their apps to a variety of data sources, including the data warehouse, emerged. The challenge, however, was the *ad hoc* nature of these connections and the way they exposed data of different meanings, structures, and timing to businesspeople who had become used to the modeled and curated approach of data warehousing.

The **logical data warehouse**, introduced by Gartner in 2011 (Beyer and Adrian, 2011), offered an overarching structure where access to relational and non-relational stores could be well integrated. These relational stores could be data marts, warehouses, or operational systems. The non-relational stores could be any file system, spreadsheet, NoSQL data store, or, indeed, any accessible system. The key component was a **semantic abstraction layer** overlying all these sources and mediating access to them. This layer hides from the users the logical and physical complexity of data with differing naming, residing in different locations and formats.

Over the following decade, the logical data warehouse was widely adopted by enterprises that had initially chosen traditional data warehousing as their preferred approach.

WEAVING A DATA FABRIC

In its simplest and most straightforward definition, **data fabric** is the current incarnation of the logical data warehouse concept. It dates to 2016 and specifically to a Forrester Wave report on "Big Data Fabric." The *Big* was replaced by *Enterprise* in the 2020 version of the report (Yuhanna, 2020), reflecting the industry-wide shift from big data to all data. A recent definition of data fabric (Ghosh, 2019) is: "a distributed data management platform, where the sole objective is to combine various types of data storage, access, preparation, analytics, and security tools in a fully compliant manner, so that data management tasks become easy and smooth." This shows the broad scope of the framework but implies there may be significant challenges in specifying it in practice.

Data fabric was listed as one of Gartner's "Top 10 Data and Analytics Trends for 2021" (Panetta, 2021). Given that logical data warehousing and data virtualization were well-known and widely implemented by then, we might reasonably ask: What is new?

The key realization of the data fabric concept is that the real-time integration of data is highly complex to define and manage over time. In a modern digital business, data sources change rapidly and often unpredictably in both content and structure. Describing and managing this requires **active metadata**—that can automatically change and grow as the environment evolves. Such active metadata can underpin AI algorithms that simplify and automate the design and operation of the system. This is achieved using advanced analytics over a **connected knowledge graph**—a deep ontology of all the information/data in the environment—stored and managed in a graph database.

In the current market, vendors fall into two broad camps. One group emphasizes the need for management of the population of the various stores. The second focuses on management of user access to these stores. This difference in weighting may be somewhat confusing, but both aspects are vital to delivery of data fabric.

The details of how this can be achieved are covered in Volume II, but it should be clear that data fabric is the obvious successor to the original concept of a "logical storehouse" of data in EBIS. But there is also a fundamental change in thinking: We now recognize that—for many reasons—not all the data required for decision-making support and analytics can be forced and funneled through a centralized, relationally based data warehouse.

So, what does this tell us?

The emergence of the logical data warehouse and its subsequent transformation to data fabric offer three lessons:

1. *Data is increasingly diverse:* The forms and structures of data of business interest is no longer confined to that which conforms to basic rows and columns. A wide range of data structures and data management approaches—including graph, hierarchical, and NoSQL, as well as text, images, audio, and video—all contribute to modern decision-making and analytical business needs. Although many such data types can be stored and lightly manipulated in RBDs, today's data warehousing must support and integrate data of many different formats residing in diverse stores.

2. *Metadata is as important as data:* Although described since the earliest days of data warehousing, metadata—data about data in the most basic of definitions[4]—has long been somewhat of a second-class citizen. Aside from its important use in contextualizing data for the business, data fabric emphasizes its vital role in data management and governance. Most importantly, we see

---

[4] As we shall see, a better name for metadata, leading to a more comprehensive definition is context-setting information (CSI).

that metadata cannot just be collected once and forgotten; it has an ongoing, active role in all aspects of managing and running a data warehousing system.

3. ***Managing data and metadata is complex:*** Every data warehouse implementer has long been aware that data management is central to all aspects of designing, building, running, monitoring, and changing a data warehousing system; and that getting it right is no easy task. Logical data warehouse and data fabric show that *metadata management* is equally important, and real-life experience shows that it is even more complex to collect, store, and manage.

The move of data warehousing to the cloud clearly adds weight to all these insights, especially to this complexity of management. Any data management workarounds or shortcuts that could be taken in on-premises implementations are unlikely to work in the cloud, due to its distributed, cross-boundary nature. In addition, the largely outsourced and shared infrastructure environment of the cloud may well constrain some aspects of required development.

BY THE DATA LAKE WE FIND A LAKEHOUSE

The next phase of our historical exploration leads us to the data lake and its successor, the data lakehouse.

Like every architecture, the original data warehouse reflected the needs and possibilities of its era. When it was designed, and until the early 2000s, by far the main source of its data was internal operational systems that managed the business processes of the enterprise. Such data is called **process-mediated data (PMD)** (Devlin, 2013) and was—and continues to be—defined, structured, and managed within the enterprise. It is the foundation for running and managing the business. It is generally well-governed and limited in scope and size[5]. The traditional data warehouse architecture, shown in *Figure 2.2*, is optimized for data with these characteristics.

The internet changed the playing field, possibly forever. By the early 2000s, new types of data blossomed in ever-increasing volumes on the internet and at its border with the enterprise. Businesses saw opportunities bloom and threats multiply. Collecting and using this data became something of an obsession, harvesting it from near-infinite clickstreams, burgeoning social media, and—more recently—the exponentially expanding internet of things (IoT). Relational

---

[5] In comparison to 21st century "big data" volumes.

databases, it was claimed, could not handle data at such size or speed at any reasonable cost. Up-front modeling must be replaced by **schema-on-read** to achieve the required speed of delivery. The data warehouse was obsolete. Most of these claims, it turns out, were exaggerated, at best. But were, at the time, accepted. Enter the **data lake**.

In a 2010 blog, James Dixon, then CTO of Pentaho, declared: "If you think of a data mart as a store of bottled water—cleansed and packaged and structured for easy consumption—the data lake is a large body of water in a more natural state. The contents of the data lake stream in from a source to fill the lake, and various users of the lake can come to examine, dive in, or take samples." (Dixon, 2010)

Throughout much of the 2010s, data lakes garnered widespread mindshare. Analysts, consultants, and vendors alike promoted the concept. Surveys early in the decade revealed that enterprises in every industry were implementing them, often declaring them—in many cases, for purely political reasons—as replacements for their existing data warehouses.

BUT... WHAT IS A DATA LAKE?

Given the watery metaphor, it may be unsurprising that the definition of a data lake has remained fluid since its inception. Gartner's definition (Gartner, 2018) is a case in point: "A **data lake** is a collection of storage instances of various data assets additional to the originating data sources. These assets are stored in a near-exact, or even exact, copy of the source format. The purpose of a **data lake** is to present an unrefined view of data to only the most highly skilled analysts, to help them explore their data refinement and analysis techniques independent of any of the system-of-record compromises that may exist in a traditional analytic data store (such as a data mart or data warehouse)."

This definition—and many more like it—of a data lake offers little of substance on which to base a solid reference architecture that would describe mandatory functions, components, interactions, and so on. "Architectures" thus range from the all-inclusive to the poetic.

At the overly comprehensive end of the spectrum, IBM defined (Chessell et al, 2015) a **data reservoir**—suggesting more engineering than a data lake. The approach emerged from multiple engagements with large enterprises, and its breadth shows clearly how many and varied are the types of data and information such enterprises store and manage. Also evident is the common desire to bring all these stores under a common set of engineering artifacts and methodologies.

The data reservoir consists of six major subsystems—data reservoir repositories, enterprise IT interaction, information integration and governance, raw data interaction, catalog interfaces, and view-based interaction—implemented through more than 30 supporting components. Within the reservoir repositories, we find raw data in sandboxes, harvested data, historical data, shared operational data, deposited data, and descriptive data; with a number of these further subdivided by source or usage[6]. The result is a system of such broad scope that it even includes IBM's Information Warehouse. Although each component is a valid candidate within a data warehousing solution, the huge scope illustrates the danger of the poorly bounded definition of the data lake: It can mean whatever you want it to.

In a more illustrative take on the data lake, Bill Inmon offers: "The data lake needs to be divided into several sections, called data ponds…: raw data pond, analog data pond, application data pond, textual data pond, and archival data pond… [which] require conditioning in order to make the data accessible and useful" (Inmon, 2016). Although phrased in less daunting terminology, the description also poses challenging design questions, such as how to define the limits of ponds within a lake. The same scoping problem is also

---

[6] The details of the data reservoir are beyond the scope of this book, but an architectural diagram can be explored at: www.slideshare.net/Hadoop_Summit/information-virtualization-query-federation-on-data-lakes [accessed 22 April 2023].

evident: A data lake can contain anything you want, in any format you need, for as long as you like. Although in this definition, conditioning is required, so the data is no longer "a near-exact, or even exact, copy of the source format," contrary to the Gartner definition quoted above.

In fact, at both ends of this spectrum, by mid-decade, extensive conditioning of data was deemed almost mandatory, in stark contrast to Dixon's original vision. This revision of the definition of data lake led directly to the data lakehouse concept discussed in *"Building the data lakehouse."*

When lakes became swamps

By 2014, numerous experts, myself included, were deeply concerned about the governance challenges of data in lakes, due to the existence of multiple, overlapping, and inconsistent copies of the same ill-defined data within them. The phrase **data swamp** (Stonebraker, 2014), (White and Heudecker, 2014), is widely used to describe this phenomenon. Providing such low-quality data is anathema to the principles of data warehousing and should not be tolerated.

On a positive note, these problems drove a new surge of interest among vendors, both old and new, in metadata, leading to a range of new initiatives and products to address the collection, management, and use of metadata in data lakes and beyond. We return to this in Volume II.

MAPPING THE DATA LAKESHORE

The origins of the data lake concept can be traced back to the advent of the web and the data flowing from its many sources—at first in streams that grew rapidly to torrents—into enterprises. From the earliest days, it was evident that a place was needed to store this raw data and analyze it at both detailed and summary levels to support business needs. It was also clear that the characteristics—usually described via the "3 Vs" of volume, velocity, and variety—of such data made it incompatible with existing data architectures and the common storage and analytic technologies of the time.

Open-source technology, such as Hadoop and associated systems, that were becoming mainstream in the early 2010s, displayed several characteristics that made it an ideal candidate to meet these storage and analytic needs. Horizontal scaling on commodity hardware offered voluminous storage and scalable processing at low cost. Because the systems were largely file-based, rather than databases, the data could be stored and processed in its raw form without the need for upfront modeling and design work. The programmatic and procedural approach to data processing (as opposed to the declarative approach at the heart of RDBs long favored by data management professionals) was attractive to the early adopters of the technology, perhaps because of their strong software programming backgrounds.

Taken together, these requirements and technology characteristics clearly indicated the need for a new, open-source software stack in the IT environment. That stack, in 2010, became the core of James Dixon's data lake.

Furthermore, as defined, the data lake was not limited to new internet-related "big data". Rather, it was increasingly applied to all data of interest to analytic users, including data traditionally processed and offered through data marts and the data warehouse. At first sight, this may appear reasonable. The analytics needed for internet-related data is similar to, although far more extensive than, that required for traditional, internally sourced data. Many applications demand that both types of data be linked together for analysis.

However, a focus on analysis needs misses key differences between these data sources. Internally sourced process-mediated data (PMD) is central to business operations and is, therefore, relatively well-governed, modeled, and intricately interlinked. The data warehouse and marts system through which it was made available to businesspeople already existed and was optimized for such data characteristics. Internet-related data is messier, poorly described, sometimes ancillary to core business processes, and comes from diverse and unrelated sources. Furthermore, although many proponents want to store it indefinitely—just in case it might be of use some time—it is generally most useful immediately and its value diminishes rapidly in the longer term.

Architecturally, these differences in usage and characteristics strongly suggest that these two classes of data are best stored and processed separately according to their differing needs, before being made available—either separately or jointly—to businesspeople for analysis and decision making. The decades-old system providing internally sourced data—the data warehouse and data marts—has proven successful, if only through its longevity. Therefore, the data lake should probably have been reserved exclusively for internet-sourced data. However, that is not the way the market developed through the 2010s.

The sexiness of new technology and the lure of cost reductions in both hardware and software led inexorably to a growing belief that the data warehouse was dead, and that all analytic and decision-making support could and should be delivered through the data lake. And as IT focus shifted to the cloud, the concept of the data lake has moved with it. However, the data warehouse has been proclaimed dead many times. To paraphrase Mark Twain's alleged riposte: "reports of its death have been greatly exaggerated." If any single concept can be said to prove this, it must surely be the emergence of the data lakehouse.

BUILDING THE DATA LAKEHOUSE

The year 2020 saw the introduction of the data lakehouse concept by Databricks, a company founded seven years earlier by the creators of Apache Spark™. According to its original description (Lorica et al, 2020), the data lakehouse is a platform that "combines the best elements of data lakes and data warehouses—delivering data management and performance typically found in data warehouses with the low-cost, flexible object stores[7] offered by data lakes." It builds on a data lake foundation because, according to the authors of a subsequent lakehouse Q&A (Armbrust et al, 2021), "today, the vast majority of enterprise data lands in data lakes" and thus they often contain "more than 90% of the data in the enterprise." Whether accurate or not, this statistic supports the wide perception that data warehouses have been subsumed into data lakes.

The lakehouse, therefore, attempts to eliminate or, at least, greatly reduce what is described as the common approach of copying subsets of that lake data to a "separate" data warehouse embedded in the lake. The reason: to support the traditional BI activities that data lake tools may struggle with.

---

[7] Early data lakes were not based on object stores, which are largely a cloud concept. The move to object storage is discussed later.

In addition, the data lakehouse focuses on real-time data streaming from mostly external sources. This contrasts with traditional data warehouses, where data was typically ingested in batches (the size of which has been decreasing as more timely data is loaded more regularly) rather than as individual records. Externally sourced data is often more variable in content and structure than internally sourced PMD. As a result, cleansing and transformation may be embedded in the streaming code rather than defined in the metadata and ETL tools used in data warehousing.

Bill Inmon has written two books on the topic: *Building the Data Lakehouse* (Inmon et al, 2021) and *The Data Lakehouse Architecture* (Inmon and Srivastava, 2022). In the former, he writes, "The unique ability of the lakehouse [is] to manage data in an open environment, blend all varieties of data from all parts of the enterprise, and combine the data science focus of the data lake with the end user analytics of the data warehouse..." This sentence confirms that the defining characteristics of a data lakehouse revolve around data management, governance, and organizational issues—exactly the same characteristics as a data warehouse.

The details of how this can be achieved are discussed in Volume II, but even the bare descriptions above lead to some possibly uncomfortable conclusions. First, the incorporation of data warehouses into data lakes over the past decade has, in many cases, been superficial at best. Second, the need for "delivering data management and performance typically found in data warehouses" clearly points to a set of business needs that demand quality data at speed for decision-making support and operational usage. This implies that the data involved must be highly structured and modeled in advance—just like PMD.

The conclusion is therefore obvious: the data lakehouse is, in architectural terms, more closely derived from the data warehouse than the data lake, although its technological foundation is more lake-like. The data lakehouse is primarily cloud-based (although some larger enterprises may run similar technology on-premises). The distinction between a data lakehouse and a cloud data warehouse thus becomes difficult to pin down precisely.

So, what does this tell us?

The emergence of the data lake and its evolution to lakehouse offers some important lessons for data warehousing on-premises or in the cloud:

1. *Data should sometimes just be left raw:* The data warehouse was built entirely on well-structured and (relatively) well-defined data. Although data mining in the 1990s allowed statistical analysis of raw, base data, it was only with the advent of internet-sourced data and the

data lake that the real value of raw data and its statistical analysis (often called analytics and now merging into machine learning and AI) became fully recognized.

2. *Governance of raw data cannot be neglected:* The common degeneration of data lakes into swamps demonstrated the significant data governance problems associated with raw data. Although this drove increased interest in metadata in the market, problems remain, and raw data governance is still challenging.

3. *Raw data must be processed for full value:* Although we can store all manner of data, we see that using raw data for analytics or decision-making support is difficult. It is often necessary to transform it into more structured forms, often relational-like, to gain its full business value.

4. *Data timeliness must be balanced with quality:* The value of external data is often highest immediately after its capture, leading to a focus on streaming data into the data lakehouse. If the metadata traditionally captured in ETL tooling is replaced by coding in the streaming environment, significant impacts on data management may ensue.

5. *Data often needs to be combined:* Early data lakes often focused solely on internet-sourced data. It soon became

clear that such data was more useful when combined with the internally sourced variety. We've learned similar lessons over and over again. The business always finds a need to join data from diverse sources together. That requirement must be anticipated and solutions that support it delivered.

The marketing blurb for the data lakehouse claims it brings the best of both warehouse and lake to the cloud. While partly true, the above observations suggest that it also brings many of the problems associated with both its predecessors.

CATCHING THE DATA MESS IN A DATA MESH

Both the data warehouse and lakehouse are founded on one key premise. In order to deliver decision-making support and analytics across the full breadth of the enterprise, some significant portion of the data must be centralized to a single store for consolidation and reconciliation. This store also offers a convenient place to build a complete historical record of the business' data as required.

Data mesh begins from a very different place. In a seminal article (Dehghani, 2019), Zhamak Dehghani proposes data mesh as an alternative to "the centralized paradigm of a lake, or its predecessor data warehouse." She lists three common and significant problems of a centralized architecture: the limited business understanding in the data preparation team, the inflexibility of centralized systems, and slow, unresponsive data provisioning. And she maintains that these problems cannot be solved in a centralized model. Her solution is "that the next enterprise data platform architecture is in the convergence of *Distributed Domain Driven Architecture*, *Self-serve Platform Design*, and *Product Thinking* with *Data*."

At the core of this definition is the concept of domain-driven design (Evans, 2003), a seemingly simple idea that the structure and language of software and its design should match the "business domain" in which it operates. The approach has been successfully applied in application development, although almost exclusively for operational applications. It has influenced the decomposition of applications into services based on business domains[8], driving the rise of the microservices architecture.

In data mesh, the domain concept is applied to data, leading to a data architecture where business units[9] take full

---

[8] It might be argued that data warehouses have also been in some sense "domain-driven." Most large organizations have multiple instances, aligned with different business domains.

[9] The term "unit" represents any organizational structure formed around a business process scope, ranging from a specific task, such as order management, to a full function, such as marketing.

responsibility for the data they need, as well as the data they deliver to other units—their "customers"—from design and creation to consumption. This leads to the ownership of data as "products" by business units. Dehghani says: "Instead of *flowing* the data from domains into a centrally owned data lake or platform, domains need to *host and serve* their domain datasets in an easily consumable way." This leads to a self-service mindset for data creation, delivery, and use.

In the data mesh approach, data products are oriented around domains and owned by independent cross-functional (in terms of their business and technical skills) teams. Each such team includes data product owners and embedded data engineers who define and deliver these data products via data pipelines that are specific to and owned by the domain. These domains use a common data infrastructure-as-a-platform to host, prepare, and serve their data assets. Dehghani describes this as "an intentionally designed distributed data architecture, under centralized governance and standardization for interoperability, enabled by a shared and harmonized self-serve data infrastructure."

Data mesh is still in the early stages of its evolution and has generated great excitement and enthusiasm in the data community. The book, *Data Mesh, Delivering Data-Driven Value at Scale* (Dehghani, 2022), offers a comprehensive overview of the architectural definition so far. Data mesh, like all such architectures, has its strengths and weaknesses, and we must await developments to see how these are balanced out in practice.

On a positive note, giving data governance a prime role is certainly a good thing. So too is the aim to address the issues of siloed data storage and delivery schemes as the analytical environment both becomes more complex in structure and demands ever more timely delivery.

However, experienced data warehouse architects may worry how data from different domains can be reconciled and made consistent, given the encapsulated nature of data products and their independent development by different teams. The traditional solution to this problem is, of course, to bring data together in an enterprise data warehouse structure, an approach explicitly excluded in Dehghani's definition of data mesh. Data fabric take another approach to the need for reconciliation. This consists of an overarching, integrated data model combined with data virtualization technology, allowing for physical consolidation as required.

Both approaches require significant up-front work to define over-arching information meaning—such as a semantic model or ontology—to ensure cross-domain interoperability. This requirement has not been discussed in any great depth so far in data mesh. The risk, therefore, may be that centralized and often inflexible data warehouses and ETL systems are to be replaced by equally inflexible siloed data domains and pipelines.

SO, WHAT DOES THIS TELL US?

Data mesh is completely novel approach to data warehousing (and recall the very broad scope in which I use the term here). It offers a chance to explore the opportunities of decision-making support and analytics, while facing up to the challenges of prior technological approaches with fresh eyes. It is, perhaps, too early to draw definitive conclusions, but there are certainly questions raised:

1. *Whither centralization in a distributed data world?* The first data warehouses envisaged centralizing all the data needed by business decision makers and analysts. Over the decades, we have gradually moved away—as we had to—from that all-or-nothing view. Data mesh proposes a complete end to centralization. Can that work?

2. *How can data be best delivered to the business?* The concept of data-as-a-product seems intuitively attractive to both businesspeople and enterprise IT data delivery teams, appearing to improve data quality and reduce IT bottlenecks. However, it is also clear that data is amorphous in many ways. How then can we define a set of products with non-porous boundaries and/or well-

managed overlap that does not create a mess of data products rather than a mess of data?

3. *How far can software engineering be applied to data?* Data mesh builds strongly on the software engineering lessons of delivering mostly operational applications in the cloud. It is often observed that the skills and methods (software engineering) appropriate for developing such apps differ from those needed to deliver decision-making support and analytics (data engineering). How much can the latter learn from the former? How far can any presumed equivalence be pushed?

Data mesh proposes a completely novel approach to data warehousing that would necessitate a comprehensive reengineering of existing environments and of development and governance methods as we move to the cloud. At best, this presents significant challenges.

DATA WAREHOUSING TODAY—IN ONE PICTURE

A picture is worth a thousand words. The following cartoon-like *"mappa mundi"* in *Figure 2.3* depicts today's data management ecosystem. Historically, this began with on-premises operational systems that run the business, feeding the EDW and data marts through traditional ETL tools for decision-making support, all within the **Land of the Enterprise**.

With the discovery of the **Big Data Ocean**, the first data lakes were dug, fed directly with external data of all sorts. Early data lakes avoided relational technology in favor of flat files and NoSQL stores, although RDBs later became popular.

Soon, the **Lake of Data** began to subsume existing data warehouses, despite being a fundamentally different concept that required more rigorous governance. A warehouse is much more than a relational database. Rather, it is a data management environment with the relational model and technology at its core. The "true" data warehouse is therefore shown residing on an **Island of Information** in the lake. This leads, of course, to many choices as to where to store both data and metadata, as well as numerous new data feeds and migration possibilities as listed in the labeled annotations.

The bridge marked **CSI / Semantic Layer** is important. It represents the evolution of metadata to a more comprehensive form—defined in *"Context-setting information (CSI)"*—and its important future role as the intermediary (semantic layer) between information and its valid use by businesspeople.

The color scheme and shading provide important information about data management and governance, which will be vital in understanding and cleaning up the mess.

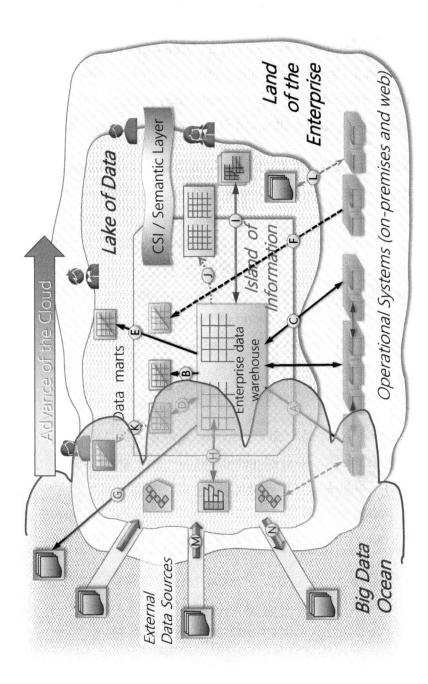

Figure 2.3: Mappa mundi of the world of data warehousing

A. EDW population (ETL)
B. Data Mart population (ETL)
C. EDW population (bi-directional)
D. Data Mart population (bi-directional)
E. Lake mart population
F. Independent mart population
G. Regulatory reporting
H. EDW population via Lake
I. Archival to Lake
J. EDW migration
K. Data Mart migration
L. Transfers of operational data to/from Lake
M. Data ingestion to Lake
N. Data export from Lake

Green cross-hatching signifies the operational processes and systems of the enterprise, producing the data—usually within business units/functions—that record and run the business. They are the sources of high-quality process-mediated data, whether originally on-premises or now on web-based apps.

Areas checkered and in shades of red are well-managed and -governed at an enterprise level, or at least across business functions. They are thus classed as information[10], and comprehensive metadata is mandatory.

Blue waves represent areas of limited or even non-existent data quality from the perspective of the enterprise. This covers all data in the data lake, as was originally conceived and, although improving in recent years, its overall quality is inconsistent at best. However well managed—by its

---

[10] Information and data are different, as explained in Chapter 3.

producers—Oceanic data may be, its passage through the internet makes it untrustworthy internally. Quality controls are therefore necessary on ingestion, particularly if or when it is landed on the Island of Information.

More recently, the cloud has been advancing rapidly from the Big Data Ocean as seen in *Figure 2.3*. From simply being the source of "data exhaust" from external systems and organizations, it is now actively treated as a valid and often preferred location and technology for all data storage and computation within the enterprise and beyond.

This is the key high-level picture to keep in mind as we explore the challenges of data warehousing in the cloud.

TAKEAWAYS

- Although the scope of business requirements and data needs has expanded considerably over the past four decades since its first appearance, the basic goal of data warehousing has remained the same: *the delivery of consistent, timely, quality, useful, and usable data for analysis and decision making by businesspeople.*

- The original data warehouse focused almost solely on delivering process-mediated data (PMD) from diverse, internal business operations with a further emphasis on building the historical record of these operations and delivering it consistently to all users.

- As timeliness increased in importance, various approaches arose to speed system development and data delivery. Of these, allowing direct, well-governed access to original data sources, in the logical data warehouse and later in data fabric, has proven increasingly popular. The distributed nature of these approaches aligns well with migration of data warehousing to the cloud.

- The explosion of interest in using externally sourced data that began arriving from the internet in vast volumes at the start of the new millennium had a radical impact on data warehousing and led directly to the concept of the data lake. This approach avoids pre-preparation of incoming data to speed delivery and allow maximum flexibility in its business analysis.

- However, data lake governance is problematical and the concept of a data lakehouse—purporting to offer the best of warehouse and lake—has recently emerged to address these concerns. In the process, it also proposes a new and expanded technological base for data warehousing in the cloud.

- The most radical approach to migrating data warehousing to the cloud is seen in the data mesh. This approach—based on experience of developing modern operational applications in a highly distributed cloud environment—shuns the use of centralized data stores and their delivery teams. Instead, it favors domain-driven development, data as a product, and distributed governance. Although highly popular as of this writing, its very different nature to traditional data warehousing thinking may prove problematical for many designers coming from current, traditional, centralized thinking.

Chapter 3

Data Warehousing—Purpose and Principles

The intelligent have plans; the wise have principles.

Raheel Farooq

Our wander down the lanes of data warehousing history was purposeful. Of the principles that we began with in the 1980s, some have remained solid in the interim decades. Some have evolved as we've better understood the needs of business and the nature of data. A few of our principles have not withstood the test of time. This chapter[11] delineates the purpose and principles of data warehousing as currently understood and how they support current business requirements.

---

[11] Parts of chapters 3 and 4 are reproduced by permission of the Insurance Data Management Association, from their Course Book, *Approaches to Data Design, Engineering, and Development* (IDMA and Devlin, 2023).

Spoiler alert: The purpose and principles of cloud data warehousing do not differ from those of data warehousing as it has existed for multiple decades.

THE PURPOSE OF CLOUD DATA WAREHOUSING

I'm using the term *cloud data warehousing* here to emphasize the forward-looking emphasis of all that follows. However, the only difference between cloud data warehousing and previous incarnations of data warehousing is that the data is being stored and processed largely or entirely off premises "in the cloud." The data storage locations and processing approaches or, indeed, any legal constraints or contractual arrangements around them can have no relevance to the business purpose intended.

The purpose of cloud data warehousing emerges from all the same reasons that drove data warehousing four decades ago. It needs repeating only because modern thinking tends to focus solely on the newest, sexiest business support technologies—analytics, predictive and prescriptive algorithms, AI, and ML—and what they offer their users. Therefore, we must keep in mind that the primary purpose of data warehousing, cloud or otherwise, is to provide the information to support businesspeople's insights in decision making and action taking. Both span from the smallest and fastest activities to the largest and slowest processes.

This purpose clearly includes the provision and preparation of the necessary data/information at the appropriate levels of timeliness, consistency, usefulness, usability, and quality, commensurate with the value offered and rigor demanded by the business activity in hand. To declare the purpose of cloud data warehousing to be solely to support "analytics"—as is often done today—is to completely underestimate the true scope of what is needed by the business and offered of the technology.

First, however, we must begin with that old conundrum—data or information—and try, once more, to put a stake in the ground. Or through data's heart ☺.

ONE LAST TIME: DATA VS. INFORMATION

Most discussions about the difference between data and information start with data and then describe why information is different. For example, data may be equated to "facts" and information defined as facts with useful context added. But what is a fact, especially in a world full of discordant opinions and fake news? Which context should be added: the context of creation, first use, or reuse? Starting the discussion with information, however, leads to far more clarity.

Information is what people create—directly (by typing or speaking into a smartphone, by taking a photograph or making a video, for example) or indirectly (such as by friending someone on Facebook, searching on Google, or researching products on Amazon). It is their means of expressing themselves and for communicating with and relating to others. Information can be anything from a poem to a purchase order, from a click trail to a call home, from an address label to an advertising video, as detailed in *Table 3.1*.

Type / Class of Information	Examples
Text	E-mail, Memos, Word-processing documents, Stories, Novels, Poems, SMS or Text Messages, Facebook posts, Tweets, Audio transcriptions, Forms (blank or filled), Field names, Descriptions and help in computer applications, Handwritten messages via optical character recognition
Audio Media	Audio recordings, Phone and VOIP calls, Music, Audio conferences, Interactions with Siri, Alexa, etc.
Video Media	Video conferences, recordings, and calls, TV programs, Movies, Virtual reality and holographic media

Type / Class of Information	Examples
Images	Photographs, Scans, Maps, Digitized drawings, Holograms
Computer Interactions	Clicks, Gestures, Selections in computer applications, Likes, Friends, and Links in social media
Future types	Emerging examples, beginning with information generated by AI, chatbots, etc.

Table 3.1: Types/Classes of Information

The examples are deliberately drawn as widely as possible from all walks of life. Not all are necessarily applicable in a business environment. However, the expansion so far in this millennium of information types used for different business purposes is instructive. It indicates that we may anticipate a growing range that piques business interest as technology enables new possibilities and society evolves.

An important characteristic of information is its **creation context**. A person who creates information does so in a certain time, place, and context, using specific tools. All of this may be relevant to the meaning or use of the information thus created. A letter written with a pencil is less durable than one written with a pen, and its content therefore deemed less reliable. A Facebook photo, stamped with date and place, may offer context of importance in a criminal case. A contract created in South Africa conforms to Roman Dutch law even though the content may not explicitly reference it. Traditional metadata represents some—mostly technical—aspects of the creation context of information.

Today, all information, almost without exception, is digitally encoded, processed, and stored either transiently or permanently in some sort of computing or communications device. The expectation is that it will be permanently available, readable, and searchable while also secure and private as required. Experience suggests that these assumptions are far less reliable than may be imagined, a fact that influences architectural decisions in many ways.

Business, information is, of course, what people (and, increasingly, AI) use to support management, analysis, decision making, and action taking throughout the organization. It should be noted that these **usage contexts** of information—and there are generally many for every set of information—most often differ from its creation context. A creation context and a set of usage contexts associated with an information set is vital to understanding, interpreting, and effectively benefiting from it.

Some context may be explicit, such as the date/timestamp and GPS location included in the metadata of a photograph. Most or all of such metadata's value and use is obvious. In contrast, implicit context may well exist in the content of the information. The use of certain slang words in a text message may offer clues to the community of the writer. The shadows in a photograph may indicate the time of day.

The next chapter will have some more to say on context, but there is a reason why it is emphasized here. Context, it turns out, is the distinguishing feature between information and data. **Naked data** is a subset of information from which context has been stripped to the maximum extent. In the simplest terms:

Information = Naked Data + Context

The qualifier *naked* is added to make clear the difference between the word *data* on its own, often used to mean different things, sometimes even to stand for *information.*

Who stripped the context away and why? It was the developers of software tools and IT applications who dropped context from information, transmuting it into naked data. In the early days of computing, they did this mainly to reduce storage and processing needs. In the 1960s, computing was generally known as *data processing,* a moniker that was literally true then and remains so in many cases today.

The approach has persisted to the present day, even though storage is now immense and processing power enormous. The reason remains largely technical. Mathematical calculations are easier when performed only on data (numbers) rather than information (contextualized numbers). A junior accountant enters sales in a spreadsheet with the currency symbol included in the cell: £30.50. As a result, monthly auto-summations fail, much to his manager's annoyance. Spreadsheets, like most applications, only deal well with naked data. When a bill is paid in Euro, however, the value of entering €50.35 becomes apparent. The summation still doesn't work, but that may be a good thing because it would be wrong. Excel would need to be a lot more sophisticated, as well as knowledgeable about exchange rates and which to apply when in order to use information (naked data qualified by currency context) rather than naked data in its calculations.

From this perspective, starting with a definition of information and deriving an understanding of data, we see that information is fundamental, while data is just a subset of it. In fact, naked data is a degenerate subset of information, degraded by the stripping away of the context explicitly or implicitly embedded in information. We must be aware that when we focus on data rather than information, we are at risk of misunderstanding or misinterpreting the meaning and relevance of the information from which that naked data was derived[12]. Furthermore—and this becomes a central pillar of all data warehousing architectures, including cloud data warehousing—we need to understand where that context goes or resides when it is sucked out of information.

The answer is surprisingly complex and varied, both logically and physically. And the cloud complicates it further. We return to this topic when we define context-setting information (CSI) in chapter 4 and explore the manifest meaning model (m^3) in depth in Volume II.

SEVEN DEADLY SINS OF DATA WAREHOUSING

Psychology tells us that we all carry unexamined assumptions from early learning and experience that color current behaviors without our conscious awareness of their power or even existence. Data warehousing experts, vendors, and implementers are no different. In my experience, there exists seven deadly sins of data warehousing—dating back many decades. They point to thinking that we unconsciously apply to design decisions, even though many of the problems they purport to address have long since been solved or mitigated.

---

[12] Throughout the rest of these books, I'll mostly use data as a shorthand for naked data for ease of reading.

1. *Never mind the information, feel the data*

We dealt with this in the previous section. Dating from the earliest days of computing in the 1950s, this category error has proven impossible to dislodge: the confusion between data and information. Its consequences persist still. Why do Chief *Information* Officers deal with technology and data management and Chief *Data* Officers with the governance of what is actually information?

2. *Operational and informational systems are separate*

Dating from the 1970s and incorporated into thinking about data warehousing from its earliest days, this remains a hidden and uncontested assumption behind many approaches to data warehousing even today.

Its origin is both business-driven and technological. Historically, decision makers operated on weekly or monthly cycles, often deliberately ignoring the daily fluctuations of business activity. On the technology front, applications were hand-crafted and run on mainframes operating at the limits of their computing power and storage. It made sense to have separate operational and informational systems: business users liked it, and anyway, the technology could not support decision-making systems running on operational databases (or files).

3. Data integration is possible only with a warehouse

In the 1980s, data warehousing was driven by the need to integrate data from disparate operational systems. These sources were often complex, poorly designed by today's standards, enormous black-box applications, built separately over many years, and never designed to work together. They could not provide a consistent view of the full business. Their data was often incomplete, inaccurate, and inconsistent across different sources. The only viable place where these problems could be fixed and data combined was the data warehouse.

4. Delivering quality data requires central control

In a direct follow-on to the previous point, such integration was only possible in a centralized location; there was no other suitably large and powerful environment at the time. No other approach was possible, and once accepted, none other was necessary to consider.

5. Layering is obligatory for speedy, easy querying

Except possibly for Teradata's massively parallel processing (MPP) warehouse, the first data warehouses of the late 1980s were exceedingly slow to deliver even simple query results, never mind the more complex queries often needed by business. Layering and subsetting of the data warehouse into an EDW and dependent data marts became almost mandatory. Although database performance improved, data volumes increased in tandem, and layering and subsetting has remained the go-to solution, despite its obvious drawbacks in development complexity and timely data delivery.

6. *An enterprise data model can exist only in the EDW*

Also in the late 1980s and into the 1990s, data modeling was becoming a popular way to translate business requirements into database structures, and the first forays into enterprise architecture and enterprise/industry data modeling were being made (Zachman, 1987), (Evernden, 1996). Given its complexity, an enterprise data model (EDM) was usually considered impossible to implement in operational systems. Performance would plunge. And the risks to daily operations were too high. The EDW (as well as master data management, MDM) was seen as an ideal environment to build out the EDM as a basis for data governance, integration, and quality.

7. *Innovative business usage of data threatens quality*

Spreadsheets became ubiquitous in the 1990s and remain businesspeople's primary data tool. IT has long regarded this as a threat to data quality. There is truth in this concern, but the innovative possibilities and ease-of-use that spreadsheets offer cannot be ignored.

This thinking is symptomatic of the central control-focused approach to data warehousing that prevailed throughout its early history. It doesn't sit well with the empowerment of businesspeople to which we aspire in digital business and cloud computing.

Each of the above postulates was valid at some stage of the evolution of data warehousing. Each and every one of them is untrue to some extent today. Some were invalidated as long as twenty years ago. However, they still cast extensive shadows in the thinking of some long-time practitioners. A brief examination of each will show where it limits current thinking and how it has led to specific design decisions in all the data warehousing approaches previously described. This rather straightforward exercise is left to the reader.

Today's practitioners also bring their own deadly sins of assumption. Theirs is a background of almost limitless computing power and storage distributed from smartphones to cloud data centers. Their software of choice is open-source, and their methodologies are Agile and DevOps. This leads to beliefs such as "decentralized everything," "Agile is the only way," or "move fast and break things." In a decade or so, these deadly sins may look as outdated as those listed above.

FIVE FOUNDATIONAL PRINCIPLES OF CLOUD DATA WAREHOUSING

Now, let's forgive ourselves of our past and present deadly sins and jump to a set of valid principles for cloud data warehousing. Principles we can be proud of today and into the future. Let's begin to define a vision of how cloud data warehousing should be. However, do keep in mind that these principles may be no more immutable than our prior sins!

One over-arching design drive is evident in digital business today. That is the desire to eliminate the functional silos and the gaps between them that emerge in every business of more than a few people. The aim is to eliminate these gaps that confuse businesspeople, slow business processes, and sow confusion and inconsistencies in data and information.

In data warehousing, our focus is on analysis, decision making, and (the oft-forgotten) subsequent action taking. Eliminating the blindingly obvious gaps between these activities in today's implementations leads to the five modern principles of data warehousing—on-premises and in the cloud.

1. **A modern digital business seamlessly combines analysis, decision making, and action taking, requiring a logically integrated, coherent continuum of *all* valid information used by the business: the** information space.

All—literally all—of the information that may potentially be used by businesspeople, irrespective of its source, is included in this information space. This incorporates all the process-mediated data produced by every operational application, whether on-premises or in the cloud. It includes all information and data received from the internet, other businesses, and regulatory authorities, as well as all information created during the processes of analysis, decision making, and action taking. This principle is emergent or evident in all modern approaches to cloud data warehousing.

But how can we know what any piece of information or data actually means and how it can be used in any specific situation? There must exist some description, which may be called *metadata*, *context-setting information*, or *ontology* of the contents of the information space.

2. **The information space must be based on a comprehensive, supra-enterprise information model, spanning *all* information types used by the business.**

The complexity and development time/cost of an enterprise data model (EDM) are familiar to traditional data warehouse implementers. Many try to minimize its role or even avoid it altogether. Nonetheless, a model spanning from semantics to logical structure is necessary to define information meaning. It must relate all information across the enterprise and address the challenges of velocity and veracity of externally sourced data.

The further implication is that the model must span enterprise boundaries—be supra-enterprise—to enable viable inter-enterprise collaboration. It must also include all types of information shared between enterprises. The need for such broad coordination of context and meaning drives industry-wide and other ontologies, but their implementation is still in its infancy.

This principle is accepted—at least theoretically—in all approaches to cloud data warehousing, except data mesh, where a more localized formulation is preferred. Implementation therefore differs by approach and will be considered on a case-by-case basis.

3. **This information space is best maintained as the minimum number of copies of each item of information, resorting only to transient layers or duplicates of specific subsets for specialized needs.**

App developers are compulsive and unapologetic copiers of existing data. It's a control thing! It removes development dependencies. It allows small (allegedly unimportant) tweaks in the data structure or content. And anyway, storage has become incredibly cheap.

But the costs of and time required for data management and information governance increase dramatically—possibly exponentially—with the number of copies and near-copies of data stored. AI may reduce this cost, although that remains unproven. The cloud's distributed nature will increase the pressure to make more copies. This is a habitual development behavior that drives technical debt. It needs to be reined in, on principle.

Thus far, the focus has been firmly on information and its storage and management. However, how is it created, modified, enhanced, delivered, and deprecated? In brief, computer processes must be developed and operated to do all these activities of managing data. This is the software needed to deliver cloud data warehousing.

4. **An integrated, model-based, and closed-loop process space is needed to create, maintain, and use information and to support human activities.**

Traditionally, data warehousing was the preserve of "data geeks" and application development the concern of "coding jockeys". In the world of data warehousing, the processes needed to manage data were often relegated to a secondary role in support of the database designers and administrators. In cloud data warehousing, this situation is no longer viable as the activities of managing data in a completely distributed environment become increasingly complex and widespread.

The processes needed to create, maintain, and use information are as important as the information itself, and modern, comprehensive software engineering practices must apply. Just as the data must be integrated, so too must be the processes around it. These processes require knowledge of the structure and meaning of the information space and thus also depend on a model-based foundation. A closed-loop approach is required to ensure that tasks that are begun will terminate properly, that their outcome is confirmed to be as expected, and if not, that appropriate steps are taken.

This leads directly to the final principle. Processes act on behalf of someone and are designed to do that person's bidding. They are what support human activity in the computing environment and that enable human access to and use of information.

5. **A supra-rational, flexible, and role-aware** people space **provides access to all process and through the process space to information.**

The real role of people and how and why they actually behave personally or in organizational roles is often largely ignored or underestimated in data warehousing and, indeed, generally in computing. This is significant because people—businesspeople, decision makers, data scientists, line workers, customers, regulators, and more—all interact with information in different roles with disparate objectives. Some of these objectives are explicit, some may be unconscious, some indeed, may be counter-productive to the business' goals, or perhaps may be illegal. People make decisions and take action; their motivations are important.

The people space addresses these vital considerations. It is often largely absent from IT considerations and cloud data warehousing thinking. Indeed, business itself hardly considers the psychological and sociological un-derpinnings of how people behave within a business mi-lieu, what motivates them, and the consequences of that—unless and until some crime is committed or some program radically fails. This principle declares that we must consider people- and organization-related aspects in the design and delivery of cloud data warehousing.

The above principles apply to all forms of data warehousing, including cloud data warehousing.

THREE THINKING SPACES FOR CLOUD DATA WAREHOUSING

The principles outlined above lead straight to a **conceptual architecture** for cloud data warehousing. The purpose of a *conceptual* architecture is to provide a shared structure and vocabulary to allow business and IT to discuss and settle on business drivers and information technology enablers. It is thus kept deliberately simple as an introductory image that both business and IT can keep in mind as they begin to discuss what cloud data warehousing means for the business and how technology drives and enables it.

This conceptual architecture was first published a decade ago (Devlin, 2013). It is uniquely based on a reevaluation from first principles of how data/information has been used in business since the beginning of data processing in the 1960s up to and including the advent in the early 2010s of data-driven business. As digital business has evolved since, this architecture—both the conceptual level described here and the logical level described in the following chapter—has so far withstood the test of time. It is thus equally applicable as a basis for designing and delivering cloud data warehousing. More recently, I have begun calling this approach the Digital Information Systems Architecture (DISA). The aim is to emphasize that this architecture can underpin all aspects of the design of and transformation to a digital business, of which cloud data warehousing is a key part.

Figure 3.1 shows the basic conceptual architecture of cloud data warehousing. The three **thinking spaces** arise directly from the spaces identified in the last section. The addition of the word *thinking* emphasizes that these are conceptual in nature; they do not show physical implementations nor even logical components. However, the spatial arrangement is meaningful. Information is placed as the foundational block; the others build upon it. Cloud data warehousing begins and ends with information. Not data, but information. Data on its own lacks the meaning and context needed as a basis for decisions or actions.

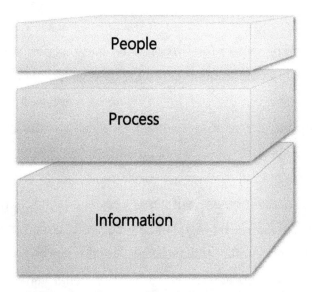

Figure 3.1: The cloud data warehousing conceptual architecture

Process is placed between people and information because people always use—create, access, or manipulate—information via some process. Processes may be formally defined and implemented or may be informal and *ad hoc* in nature. However, no matter how loosely defined, we recognize that using information is a process that can be modeled, managed, and improved as needed.

Finally, people—whether individually or collectively in organizational units—are the primary drivers of everything in the digital business. The people thinking space therefore sits above the other two blocks.

Also called the IDEAL architecture, the acronym lists its five key aspects: Integrated/Inclusive, Distributed, Emergent, Adaptive, and Latent. These characteristics are largely self-explanatory, except for *latent*, confirming that this conceptual view remains hidden in the logical architecture and implementation as we see later. This name emphasizes that a conceptual architecture is, in fact, an ideal that can only be approached but never perfected. In business and IT, trade-offs are always necessary. Furthermore, in a constantly changing environment, business needs and technical possibilities are always evolving, and an ideal must accommodate that. The conceptual architecture is therefore more an image of what we aim to achieve rather than what can be fully delivered. Further details can be found in *Business unIntelligence* (Devlin,2013).

You might argue that technology should also appear here. Indeed, there are long-standing methodologies for strategic planning that include technology, either instead of or in addition to data/information (Simon, 2021), (Shevlin, 2021). Technology does play a role in conceptual architecture, and could certainly be depicted as a fourth thinking space beneath information. However, in my experience, architects are often too focused on technology and may overemphasize it in discussions with the business. I therefore made a conscious decision to exclude it at this level of architecture, knowing that IT will bring their knowledge of it to the conversation anyway. I generally reserve consideration of technology to the physical implementation stage of design.

Figure 3.1 is kept deliberately simple as the initial starting point of the business-IT conversation. When we need to dive to the next level of conceptual thought, we add to each thinking space a set of three axes as shown in *Figure 3.2*. Each axis represents a topic of significant importance in the discussion between business and IT, as experienced over the years of designing data warehousing solutions.

The choice of three axes is, again, driven by the goal of keeping the picture clear and simple, both in its representation and in its discussion. However, in a specific implementation, additional or other topics may rise in importance and need to be added to the picture or to replace/extend the existing axes. The individual axes, particularly those of the information space, will be considered in more depth as we explore each of the three thinking spaces.

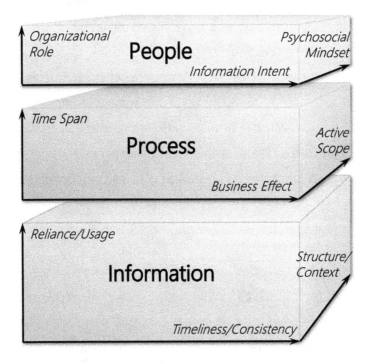

Figure 3.2: The axes of the conceptual thinking spaces

THE INFORMATION THINKING SPACE

The information thinking space is a conceptual view of the *entire* information resource of the enterprise—whatever its source, structure, or storage—that the business uses or may use to achieve its goals. Such information may reside in the data center, the cloud, on personal computers, smartphones, or any network-attachable device with computing function—in short, anywhere. The information may be formally the property of the enterprise or belong to its customers or partner enterprises, such as social media firms, governments, and so on. This inclusion of *all* information—whatever its location or ownership—is necessary because a modern business uses a much broader scope of data/information than traditional businesses and implicitly depends on the availability and quality of all that information.

The three axes of the information space represent key conversations between business and IT, as well as vital trade-offs that must be made in delivering cloud data warehousing. Although it might be argued that there should be more than three topics, experience shows that the chosen axes and their composite character are generally as far as business will want to go and as deep as IT needs to delve to determine the most important design considerations.

As shown in *Figure 3.3*, each axis is labeled with a series of classes, indicating the state of the information at those positions. For example, on the timeliness/consistency axis, we have a series of classes that would be familiar to a data warehouse architect: live information is found in operational systems; reconciled in data warehouses; etc.

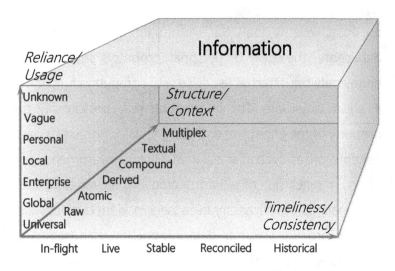

Figure 3.3: The three axes of the information thinking space

The idea is that a piece or set of information is positioned in the three-dimensional space based on the characteristics that can be read off the axes. However, all three axes are continua and the classes depicted are not discrete steps. When we identify information along some axis, we may find that it has some characteristics of two or more classes.

The Timeliness/Consistency Axis

In a digital business, with data coming at speed from multiple sources, understanding the trade-off between timeliness and consistency for any resulting information set is vital. If all the data needed comes from one source, its timeliness and thus the speed at which it can be processed is set only by that source, which also determines how internally consistent it is.

With multiple sources, however, consistency must be ensured after all the source data is available. This determines the timeliness of the information seen by the business. In addition, the faster the required reconciliation, the more expensive it is. The classes on this axis are largely self-explanatory, ranging from the timeliest and most transient on the left to the most consistent and permanent on the right.

The Structure/Context Axis

Big data is often described as *unstructured* or *semi-structured* in comparison to the *structured* data found in traditional systems. The terminology is unfortunate. Unstructured data cannot exist; that is just noise. However, the extent of structuring of data is an important characteristic that determines how it can be stored and processed. For example, the highly structured atomic data in an order entry system or that used to manage the business in a data mart is very different from the loosely structured information in a textual contract or in the multiplex videos or images on Facebook.

The related and, arguably, more important characteristic included on this axis is the context that is embedded with the data and makes it usable and useful for the business. Raw data, coming from sensors, for example, is just numbers. It requires extensive metadata and descriptions before it can be understood and safely used. The multiplex information of a video recorded at the scene of an accident, on the other hand, contains a wealth of context that a human (or increasingly an AI system) may be able to extract without explicit metadata. Raw data is encoded and has a meaning and minimal structure that is defined by its designer, while multiplex information is more loosely structured with implicit/tacit meaning and context.

The balance of these two aspects—structure and context—of any information required or used by the business provides specific storage and processing requirements to IT and drives technology choices and implementation approaches.

The Reliance/Usage Axis

The third axis shows the level of trust that the business can place in information and how safely it can be used. The classes on this axis range from completely trustworthy, universally usable information to that which has unknown provenance and can only be used with great care. Enterprise information, for example, in an EDW, can be used across the entire organization. Global information can be shared with other organizations or regulators. At the other end of the spectrum, personal information (in spreadsheets, for example) and vague information, such as that arriving from YouTube, requires careful identification, management, and possibly restricted access within the enterprise.

Cloud implementation of data warehousing may lead to new considerations on this axis compared to on-premises implementations. This may occur when locating specific types of data/information in the cloud gives rise to varying reliance/usage considerations. For example, in the case of personally identifiable information (PII), the location or jurisdiction where data is stored gives rise to various legal and sovereignty issues that would appear on this axis.

THE PROCESS THINKING SPACE

The process thinking space for cloud data warehousing, shown in *Figure 3.3*, positions **tasks** or types of activities to better understand their key characteristics. As in the case of the information thinking space, the classes are a continuum, merging from one to the next, rather than discrete divisions. The process space is somewhat simpler than its information counterpart; each axis here represents a single characteristic.

The first process dimension is **active scope**, which is based on microservices—and originally, Service Oriented Architecture (SOA)—thinking. The lowest level is an **event** in the real world. This might be a simple machine sensor measurement or a basic value calculation. It might be a communications event, such as a tweet or an email. Legally significant events or combinations thereof take on special significance and become **transactions** through cleansing and validation.

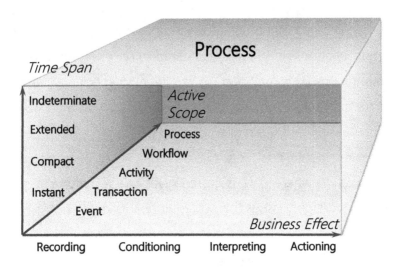

Figure 3.4: The three axes of the process thinking space

An **activity**, or service in SOA, is the smallest unit of function that makes sense to a business user, usually consisting of a number of related transactions and events. Services are defined by the business but implemented by IT to maintain internal consistency. A **workflow** links activities into flexible sequences as workflows. These are defined by businesspeople and may be implemented or changed by them, at least in principle. A **process** is the highest level of workflow delivering a value-generating set of interdependent activities.

The **business effect** dimension describes how any action taken relates to the underlying business information. **Recording** is the act of capturing any class of data/information from any source. This ranges from storing it in a database—where a permanent record is necessary—to simply "noting" in-flight data or accessing it remotely. Metadata is also recorded.

Conditioning covers all subsequent changes to, calculations about, and derivations and deletions of the recorded information. *Interpreting* is the next step of applying intelligence to information to understand its business implications. It is thus a function found in both operational and informational systems. It ranges from validating and understanding the data entered to analytics. Finally, *actioning* reaches a decision on what to do and taking the appropriate action.

Time span represents the period of time over which a process element is active or open. The *instant* time span, associated only with events and the simplest of transactions, refers to the shortest measurable timing. Each such event or transaction deals with a single, integral piece of information. Operational transactions occur in a *compact* time span, a period of time within which a person might place an order for an item, for example. The *extended* time span recognizes that some activities can spread over hours, days, or more because of temporal dependencies either in the real world— closing a contract—or in the technical environment—running a batch job. The *indeterminate* time span applies to processes that could possibly go on forever and where no end condition can be defined. Business processes at the highest level have this characteristic.

THE PEOPLE THINKING SPACE

The people thinking space provides the foundation for understanding why and how businesspeople use and process information to drive business needs, to get their job done, and to succeed in their roles. In defining cloud data warehousing today, it is—unfortunately—given the least attention, simply because current technologies seldom consider these matters too deeply.

Figure 3.5 shows the three axes and their ranges of characteristics that must be considered.

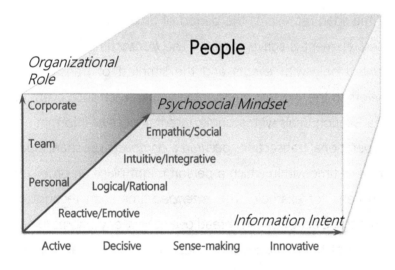

Figure 3.5: The three axes of the people thinking space

Organizational role is the most familiar and simplest axis. People use information and make decisions aligned to their role in the organization, which is shown here in a typical but generic hierarchical structure.

The **information intent** axis provides the primary linkage from the people space to the spaces below it. *Active* intent—getting something done—is the simplest and most common motivation in business, especially in day-to-day operations and in time-constrained activities. It is supported through operational applications and operational BI. *Decisive* intent—reaching a decision—is seen most obviously in people the organization empowers to make decisions of significance: managers and executives. This is the most common area for application of traditional BI and dashboarding tools.

Sense-making intent is the behavior of seeking a story to explain some phenomenon and what to do about it. BI tools, as well as analytics—and spreadsheets—are most often applied here. Intuition and team working, with its social and empathic skills, are required. Significant expansion in IT support is needed here, driven by the recognition that human behavior is far more complex and nuanced than business typically imagines. *Innovative* intent drives the "ah-ha moments", the creation of novelty, the spark for new products or processes. It is the least understood, most poorly supported, and least managed of all four types of intent. It is the source of the most important behaviors and requires future business and IT focus.

Perhaps the most interesting and, sadly, least often considered aspects of business use of information and decision making lie on the **psychosocial mindset** axis. Much of academic and business school consideration of business decision making starts—and ends—with **rational decision theory** (March, 1994), which is a poor basis for understanding how real people behave, especially under stress.

Modern psychology and neurobiology show that—in real life—much more is involved. This leads to the concept of **insightful decision making** that is well-informed but cognizant of the decision maker's mental landscape. Combining left and right brain, it takes account of intuitive and emotional concerns to reach integrated, well-rounded decisions (Siegel, 2010). Human behavior operates at all psychosocial levels and applies also to decision making in business settings.

At the lowest level, *reactive/emotive* impulses may be unconscious, driving actions that may not be in the best interests of the business or the person. Such impulses cannot be eliminated; rather, the goal is to integrate the negative and positive aspects to create more holistic functioning. *Logical/rational* thinking is so deeply embedded in Western culture that we imagine it to be the most desirable and prevalent mode of thinking. Both are myths. While vital for many tasks, logic alone can miss the bigger picture and come to distinctly inhuman conclusions, a danger becoming apparent in emerging horror stories from the application of AI to social problems (O'Neill, 2016).

In the right brain, *intuitive/integrative* thought sees the forest for the trees and finds those "ah-ha insights". This is the source of creativity and the mother of invention. Working together with the structured and rational left brain, this drives the creativity that modern business seeks. Finally, *empathic/social* thought is the foundation of relating at the personal, group, and societal levels. Collaboration springs from here, and with it, our best opportunities for innovation.

Further academic research and development are needed to elaborate this thinking space and allow it to take its proper and vital role in future cloud data warehousing design.

TAKEAWAYS

- The purpose of cloud data warehousing is the same as that of data warehousing in general. This purpose is to enable and support businesspeople in their analysis, decision making, and action taking required to run and manage the business. It provides them with the data and information they need at suitable levels of timeliness, consistency, usefulness, usability, and quality, commensurate with the value offered and the rigor demanded by the business activity in hand.

- Information is what the business needs from cloud data warehousing. Data, stripped of context to varying degrees, is not sufficient.

- Examining the history of data warehousing shows seven mistaken or outdated assumptions that may underpin poorly considered decisions about the scope of cloud data warehousing, what it can achieve, and its fundamental limitations.

- The five foundational principles of cloud data warehousing set its scope as *all* the information that may be used by the business and the processes needed to deliver and manage that information. People are positioned as the ultimate arbiters of what is to be delivered.

- The three thinking spaces of the conceptual architecture of cloud data warehousing are information, process, and people, with information as the foundation and people at the apex. Each thinking space provides the basic design topics that must be discussed and agreed between the business and IT.

- These same three spaces allow us to tell the simplest and most elegant story of the purpose of cloud data warehousing: *People process information.*

Chapter 4

Cloud Data Warehousing Logical Architecture

We learn from history that we do not learn from history.

Georg Hegel

Under cover of the cloud, novel and subtle architectural shifts are taking place. Very little of this is visible in the previous chapter, where we described the conceptual architecture for cloud data warehousing. After all, the purpose and principles of data warehousing remain the same irrespective of the physical location of your information or the ownership of the computers where it's stored and processed. Foggy thinking about the cloud obscures the fact that storage and processing remain stubbornly earthbound or, at least in physical computers—such as your smartphone—that may be flying around the world or embedded in every variety of static or mobile infrastructure.

Now, as we move from the conceptual level, it is in the logical architecture that we must face the consequences of storing data in an increasingly distributed fashion; of managing information across time zones, political borders and jurisdictions, and organizational boundaries; and processing business needs within the new technological possibilities and limitations of the cloud. A logical architecture bridges the gap between the ideals of what the business desires and the technological choices that IT will make to try to satisfy them. That is the bridge we cross in this chapter.

We start by translating the ideas of the information thinking space into concrete terms by simplifying information into three (and a half) distinct and identifiable domains. This leads to the concept of information pillars, as opposed to the layered thinking of more traditional data warehousing.

Next is the logical process architecture, where closed-loop approaches and modern software methods allow us to identify the basic types of function required to support the creation and management of information across these pillars.

There is no logical people architecture. We hesitate to architect or design the human mind or heart! However, organizational concerns and limitations appear throughout the logical architecture, to which we will certainly return in Volume II.

Logical architectures represent the technical functionality and methods we require, irrespective of whether particular versions of specific products support them today. Knowing the required function, an implementer can evaluate products for compliance. This is the essence of architecture. Product vendors may call currently offered high-level function "architecture," but this is confusing and should be avoided.

And, finally, it is in the logical architecture that we begin to distinguish between on-premises, cloud, and hybrid implementations of data warehousing.

INFORMATION DOMAINS AND TYPES

The starting point for defining the information components of the logical architecture is to examine how different commonly used types of data/information are distributed in the information thinking space. *Figure 4.1* shows three such types: the data warehouse, internet of things (IoT), and social media. Even the most general understanding of their characteristics—based on the axes of the information space—shows that they are positioned in different parts of the space.

From this, we infer that distinct types of data/information exist in the modern business and that their different characteristics often demand different technologies and/or methods to create and manage them. The chosen types correspond to the three main domains of data/information introduced next, although in the real world, of course, overlaps do exist.

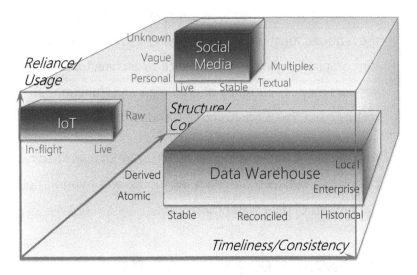

Figure 4.1 Positioning types of data in the information space

THE TRI-DOMAIN+ INFORMATION MODEL

Figure 4.2 shows the three domains[13]—process-mediated data, machine-generated data, and human-sourced information—and their inter-conversions in two dimensions of the information thinking space. The "+" is context-setting information, which links the three domains together. For simplicity, the reliance/usage axis has been omitted because

---

[13] Not to be confused with domain as used by data mesh in "domain-driven design," here simply a distinct set of data/information.

information domains are less dependent on reliance/usage considerations, but they will be noted where appropriate.

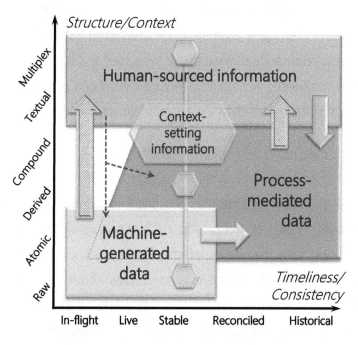

Figure 4.2 The tri-domain+ information model

Careful consideration shows that all the domains definitions are independent of where they physically exist: on-premises, in the cloud, or some hybrid combination of both. They are all equally at home and equally relevant on any platform. There are, of course, implementation considerations related to the highly distributed nature of the cloud. These are reflected later in *"Cloud formation in pillars."*

PROCESS-MEDIATED DATA (PMD)

Throughout much of the computing era and up to the end of the last century, almost all the data used and needed to run and manage a business originated from data entry into internal operational systems, as discussed in Chapter 2. Today, businesses increasingly require clients and prospects to input much of this data via web and smartphone apps.

Such data has rather special characteristics. The designers of such data entry apps, wherever located, ensure that the data is as clean and consistent as possible through specific screen layouts, choice of fields, and data-checking algorithms. In addition, they may be supplemented by data-entry or data-onboarding staff trained in arcane rules about valid structures and content of data that is input. The resulting class of data is called **process-mediated data (PMD)** because its collection and creation have been well-managed in the input, checking, and derivation processes.

Some may criticize the quality of implementation. However, when best practices are followed, such data is the gold standard in recording the reality of what the enterprise is doing to achieve its formal and stated business goals. If an order is not recorded in PMD, it has no legal standing and might as well not exist. Further examples of PMD include customer details, inventory records, and account transactions.

Account balances are examples of derived PMD. Some PMD comes from external organizations, such as credit scores and tax rate data. In addition, PMD created within one business may be sent to regulators and other organizations where it becomes core to their internal processes. In terms of reliance/usage, PMD spans the range from local to global and is particularly important in the enterprise class.

Beyond on-premises implementations, PMD is now mostly created in cloud-based apps, as well as on web pages on the internet, and smartphone apps. It is vitally important that similar quality, control, and security processes apply in onboarding data in these cases as was applied for on-premises data entry. If not, the resulting PMD is of lower quality in terms of reliance/usage. It may thus need further cleansing and improving, or be subject to limitations in use.

MACHINE-GENERATED DATA (MGD)

Since the turn of the century, the other two classes of data/information have grown significantly in importance. The first is **machine-generated data (MGD)**, which is exactly what the name says. This data was previously the preserve of specific industries, such as manufacturing, telecoms, or utilities, where it was created in well-managed conditions under the strict control of the owning enterprise, often in collaboration with its technology vendors. Banks had their first experience of such data, also internally controlled, with the emergence of automated teller machines (ATMs) in the 1980s. Such MGD exists at the local and enterprise levels of reliance/usage.

More recently, MGD has become ubiquitous across many more industries as the internet of things (IoT) has grown exponentially. Although largely identical in structural terms to internally sourced MGD, its origins in the IoT cause additional and significant concerns about its reliance and usage: it generally exists first at the vague level (see *Figure 3.3*). Automobile insurers, for example, may rely on telematic data from on-board computers. The quality of such raw MGD may be compromised in many ways. The sensors or computer in the automobile may have been modified. On its passage through the internet, it may have been intercepted and hacked. If the raw telematic data has been pre-processed by a third-party provider, however, the resulting cleansed data is positioned at the local or enterprise levels of reliance/usage by that intermediary. Further processed and (possibly) summarized data passed to the insurer may then be properly considered and treated as PMD by them.

Given its external sourcing, such MGD is likely to be first ingested, (pre-)processed, and stored in the cloud, making it a prime candidate for early cloud data warehousing implementation. As seen in the above example, the reliance/usage aspects require careful consideration.

HUMAN-SOURCED INFORMATION (HSI)

The final class of data/information is **human-sourced information (HSI)**. In contrast to the previous two classes, this is information rather than data; it is contextually rich and loosely structured. It consists of everything from tweets to videos, poems to legal contracts, songs to voice messages, all of which people create to describe their world and communicate with one another.

Although HSI has been around in some form since time immemorial, its direct use in information systems has grown to significant and computationally useful levels with the advent of social media. Prior to this, although businesses had commonly stored HSI—the content of contracts or e-mails, for example—the type and extent of processing possible was limited. As in the case of MGD, the sourcing—internal or external to the enterprise—of human-sourced information is an important factor in determining how it should be stored and managed, and its positioning on the reliance/usage axis varies accordingly. Social media ranges from unknown to personal, whereas contractual information is likely to be placed at the enterprise level (see *Figure 3.3*).

HSI spans all industries. Insurance offers some interesting examples. Externally sourced HSI include photos and scanned, hand-drawn diagrams submitted in claims, as well as online chats or emails with claimants or others in the process. Insurance policies are examples of internally generated HSI. Note, however, that such documents are built in part on the PMD generated by premium calculation systems. The distinction revolves around the uses made of the different parts of the document. The textual content—HSI—sets the human-interpretable context that may be argued later in a court of law; the PMD is used by the insurance processes to bill premiums, and so on. Similar considerations apply to other industries.

Context-setting information (CSI)

Spanning and overlying the HSI and PMD domains is **context-setting information (CSI)**. Its positioning indicates its nature is compound and textual in terms of structure/context and live/stable/reconciled on the timeliness axis. CSI does simply and exactly what it says: it is information that sets the context for, well, everything. Its applicability to HSI, PMD, and MGD is indicated by the small matching, connected hexagons in each domain. CSI therefore far exceeds the scope of the commonly used term, *metadata* (often defined simply as data about data). It describes (in a physical computing medium) what everything is and does, providing the background to each piece of data or information, to every process component, and all the people that constitute and are involved in the business.

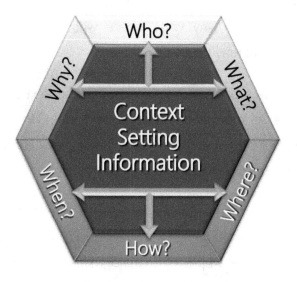

Figure 4.3: Context-setting information

Context, as shown in *Figure 4.3*, includes everything you need to know when creating or using a piece of information. Its meaning is expressed primarily in the three questions at the top of the hexagon—what the information is, why it is of interest, and to whom. The three questions in the lower half of the hexagon provide the details of how it is represented and where, as well as the various constraints of time of applicability, storage, or usage.

In each area, we can dive as deep as needed to discover details of the storage location and structure of data/information, its lineage and provenance, who owns it or manages it, why it is important and where it can be safely used, and more. CSI spans a similar scope for process and people, answering all the why, what, where, who, when, and how questions that may be asked.

In truth, every piece of information adds context to something else. All information is thus context-setting to a greater or lesser extent—one of the reasons why metadata projects have proven so difficult to scope and complete.

CSI is, in essence, the glue that holds the entire scope of data warehousing together. It is stored and communicated semantically, for example, in a catalog, knowledge graph, or similar tool, and must be made available and managed in a fully distributed manner, given that it must span multiple and differing information and data classes.

The creation and ongoing management of context-setting information lies at the core of data fabric—particularly in the automation of the information preparation systems. We thus explore CSI in more depth in Volume II before unraveling the warp and weft of data fabric.

TRI-DOMAIN+ MODEL TRANSFORMATIONS

Referring again to *Figure 4.2,* we note that all these domains of data/information are shown to overlap to varying extents and can be inter-converted via the overlaid arrows. The overlaps signify the flexibility of this model in defining the domains. The arrows show how data and/or information can be transformed between them.

Both MGD and HSI can be converted into PMD (the solid arrows) by applying appropriate transformation and quality assurance procedures. These processes represent the creation (or modification) of legally binding business transactions involved in running and managing a business.

PMD and MGD can create HSI (the cross-hatched arrows) using, for example, BI and visualization tools to create reports and graphics to communicate data to people. These processes support decision making and other management activities. In the opposite direction, the narrow, dashed arrows from HSI indicate that MGD and PMD are first defined and described by people via HSI.

These arrows and overlaps between the domains indicate that data and information in their three forms represent a complex and interrelated ecosystem where each type begets another. However, this certainly does *not* mean that the three domains can be collapsed into one. Their structure, as well as storage, processing, and quality needs, are distinct and deserving of separate consideration in any self-respecting data/information architecture.

The urge to consider all domains as the same is especially powerful as data warehousing moves to the cloud, along with the move toward a single underlying storage structure (object store), as discussed in *"Cloud formation in pillars."* This is a temptation that should be strongly resisted. These domains have very different governance, management, and processing characteristics that must be maintained irrespective of raw data storage choices.

INTRODUCING INFORMATION PILLARS

As we continue to transition from a conceptual representation to functional considerations in the logical architecture, we adopt another representation of these three domains, as shown in *Figure 4.4*, to represent some additional and important design aspects.

In this figure—which is the first step in drawing the logical level of the cloud data warehousing architecture—each domain is represented by a **pillar** of data/information with a similar set of characteristics. This represents an initial high-level design choice to store and manage each data/information domain in a similar manner, using similar technology, and even physically collocated, whether on-premises or in the cloud. Meanwhile, context-setting information (CSI) spans all three pillars, indicating its key role in holding them together and relating each to the other.

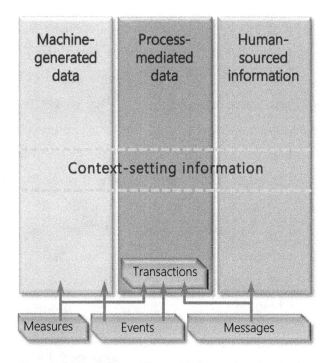

Figure 4.4 The three pillars of information (basic view)

Data and information flow upward in these three pillars according to the convention that puts people at the top of the picture, as in the conceptual architecture.

Data and information are shown as coming originally from *actions* in the real world: physical **events** (for example, a switch is thrown) and **measures** (such as the current temperature) recorded by sensors and machines, and **messages** (from tweets to videos) created by people. Different actions end up in different pillars depending on what they convey and what use the business makes of them.

A key point is that when any real-world actions arrive in the PMD pillar, they are first converted to **transactions**. A transaction is a legally binding record of some action of significance to the enterprise, and it is this that makes process-mediated data special. The word *transaction* is used here in a different sense to that in databases. Here, its significance is in its legal status as a complete, permanent (subject to data retention considerations) record of a business event as it is understood and agreed at that moment. Transactions cover contract and account creation, orders, claims, deliveries, address setting, product prices, and definitions—in fact, any significant, binding element of data on which business operations depend. The creation of transactions demands proper governance and strict management because the PMD thus created is the basis of the business' financial and legal obligations. As a result, PMD demands significantly higher levels of data quality than most instances of MGD or HSI.

That is not to suggest that data/information governance is not important in the other pillars. It is. However, it can be applied more lightly and at a lower cost, unless the data in question may have significant impact on health, security, and other critical areas. Furthermore, where MGD or HSI is the foundation of digital products offered to customers, additional governance and management will be required.

We may expect data and information to flow more swiftly and freely in these two pillars. Its use may be expedited or more widely allowed, although data governance must ensure that the business is mindful that their quality and consistency cannot be relied upon to the same extent as for PMD.

PILLARS VS. LAYERS VS. SILOS

Contrast these pillars with the **layers** common in traditional data warehouse architectures, where data is forced to traverse each layer in sequence until it reaches its users. Each layer has, of course, a valid purpose: to transform, cleanse, integrate, subset, or otherwise manipulate the data. However, each layer demands another copy of the data and another set of preparation function to create it. These layers of data and function add complexity to the design and management of data and software. In operation, they delay the arrival of the data at its final destination, its users. Of course, some layering will be necessary in specific circumstances, but the pillared approach here reflects the third principle of cloud data warehousing—minimizing copies of information—described in *"Five foundational principles of cloud data warehousing."*

Some readers may question how pillars differ from the dreaded silos of data that app developers regularly introduce and that data warehousing has long tried to avoid. The simple answer is that pillars are *designed* to interoperate, whereas silos are strictly stand-alone by design and/or implementation. The interoperability of pillars depends first on the CSI that spans them. It is CSI that describes the semantics and defines the relationships between the pillars. For example, the link in CSI between a social media ID in HSI and a customer number in PMD (where legally permitted) allows the data and information to be joined. As seen in the following section, *"Fleshing out the function,"* a specific function, assimilation, in the process space is defined to create and manage these components of CSI.

PILLAR PARTITIONING

Figure 4.5 is a more complete view of the logical information architecture, where each pillar is decorated by a couple of icons representing types of data storage, as well as a dashed vertical divider. The implication is that in any real-world implementation, a pillar may be further divided into two (or more) parts if the characteristics of the data/information and its business use suggest that such a division may be functionally useful.

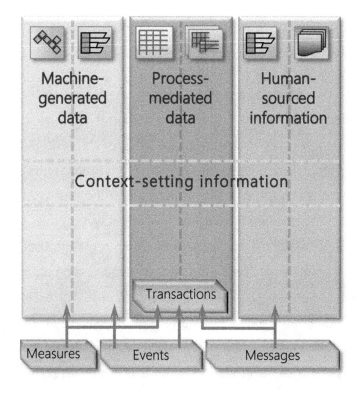

Figure 4.5 The three pillars of information (full view)

For example, MGD coming from an enterprise's own production line is more reliable than that coming from external data sources, such as poorly maintained sensors in a fleet of third-party delivery trucks. Storing, managing, and processing them differently may make sense. Similarly, HSI from your own call center logs and transcripts is of a different structure, speed, and quality than that coming from Twitter. Again, the design questions revolve around physical and quality characteristics of the data/information, as well as its use, and lead to differing data management considerations.

We must also be aware of the implications of the earlier conceptual-level definition of the information thinking space as "the *entire* information resource of the enterprise." It is tempting to imagine all these pillars of information residing within the IT systems of the enterprise. In the past, such an interpretation might have been valid. However, this is no longer true. Increasingly, some of the information used by the enterprise may belong to another organization and may be accessed only as needed by the enterprise. For example, analyzing social media posts and relationships may be a key part of managing churn. Such information is clearly part of the enterprise information resource and specifically found within HSI. However, its storage and legal ownership remain with the social media provider, and a significant portion of this enterprise HSI is thus beyond the using enterprise's boundaries. This leads to data management and governance approaches that will be based on contractual service delivery agreements between the enterprise and the social media provider allowing information to be accessed as required by the requesting enterprise but not stored internally.

CLOUD FORMATION IN PILLARS

The tri-domain+ information model is largely agnostic to the location of information—be it on-premises, in mainframes or smartphones, or in the cloud—except in its consideration of the reliance/usage axis. As discussed in the previous section, reliance/usage impacts the three domains differently and the implications of the varying levels of management and governance implied by the classes on this axis must be considered carefully.

In cloud data warehousing, some or all of the enterprise's information resides in the cloud. However, it should be clear that information stored in the cloud may also exhibit differing levels of management and governance, ranging from highly regulated enterprise-quality data to "sandboxes" for personal use by data scientists. Data sourced from across the internet retains its vagueness (as a class of reliance/usage) whether it is ingested into on-premises or cloud storage.

From these deliberations, we conclude that no new pillars of information are needed in cloud data warehousing. Rather, the thinking that led to vertically partitioning each pillar based on technology and management/governance considerations can fully support cloud and hybrid, as well as on-premises, implementations.

However, two broad aspects of cloud implementation lead to an extension of the representation of the information pillars for cloud, as shown in *Figure 4.6*.

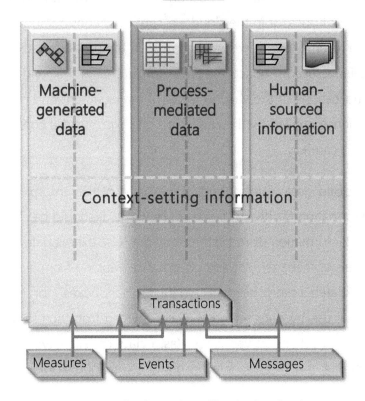

Figure 4.6 Information pillars in the cloud

At the highest level, each pillar may exist on-premises and/or in one or more cloud environments. The two **information planes** in the figure show that an enterprise may store data/information in two (or more) cloud environments, such as AWS and Microsoft Azure. This approach is widespread, whether by accident or design, and is generally known as

multicloud. The addition of multiple planes to the logical architecture also allows the depiction of distributed cloud, regions, edge computing, and other highly distributed options. The on-premises environment would simply be a third plane, structured as shown previously in *Figure 4.5*.

In a more obvious change, the pillars in *Figure 4.6* are all joined at the foot. This represents a strong trend in cloud technology to base data and information management on object storage technology, such as AWS S3, Microsoft Azure Blob Storage, and Google Cloud Storage. Object storage, dating to the mid-1990s, is often associated with "unstructured" information (for a discussion of this term, see *"The Structure/Context Axis"*). It departs from traditional block and file storage of data, allowing huge binary objects to be stored and accessed, usually via globally unique identifiers across multiple hardware instances, directly via application programming interfaces (APIs). Object stores are optimized for write-once / read-many access and are ideal for storing or archiving large multiplex objects such as video, images, audio, and text.

However, because objects also allow storage of significant amounts of technical and structural metadata, data structures can be constructed within them, supporting opensource data formats, such as Apache Iceberg, Parquet, and ORC. These formats have become the preferred base for cloud data warehousing implementation, despite limited native support for maintaining a single, accurately updated version of the data. These limitations restrict the use of such formats in operational systems and additional workarounds are required to support streaming or real-time data ingestion in cloud data warehouses and data lakehouses.

The ability of object stores to handle (with varying levels of ease and elegance) multiple data/information classes offers the possibility of a common base storage platform supporting all pillars, as shown in *Figure 4.6*. However, optimized storage formats from relational and graph databases to wide-column stores and, indeed, flat files, continue to be required, as shown in the pillar structure that is retained at the higher level in the image.

Based on the above, we can see that a cloud data warehousing architecture consists largely of technology specializations of the generic data warehousing architecture first defined in the on-premises era. This allows us, in Volume II, to directly map data lakehouse and data fabric to the architecture being unfolded here. The reason is that both these approaches emerge directly from the original data warehouse architecture described earlier in *"Enter the data warehouse."* Mapping to data mesh is more problematical, as we shall see, because of its focus on data-as-a-product, which leads to the reduction or elimination of the differences between the three data/information domains defined here. The pros and cons of this exclusion are discussed in Volume II.

FLESHING OUT THE FUNCTION

With the information pillars defined, we can now explore the processes and function needed to create, maintain, and use them. With this, the full extent of the logical architecture emerges. Its goal is to provide a comprehensive—but as far as is practicable, product-agnostic—map of the functionality needed to implement cloud data warehousing.

The full logical architecture is shown in *Figure 4.7*. Its key characteristics are expressed in its acronym, REAL in *Business unIntelligence*, which was, of course, chosen to contrast with the idealization inherent at the conceptual level. REAL stands for Realistic, Extensible, Actionable, and Labile[14].

As previously mentioned, the logical architecture does not include a people-related component. However, the *conceptual* people space has been added to the diagram to emphasize that all the logical information and function exist solely to support businesspeople in decision making and action taking across all areas of interest. It also highlights that people are the source of the messages that occur at the base of

---

[14] *Labile* is a synonym for flexible.

the logical architecture. (Measures and events emerge from the physical world of sensors and computing devices.)

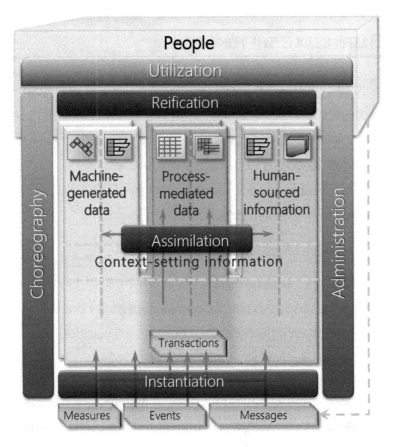

Figure 4.7 The full logical architecture of cloud data warehousing

At the center of the architecture are three information preparation functions: instantiation, assimilation, and reification[15].

---

[15] "The process of making something abstract more concrete or real." (Philosophy) *The New Oxford Dictionary of English*

These functions gather the outputs of real-world actions (events, measures, and messages), convert them into usable and useful information, and make it available to the business as a foundation for decisions and actions taken by (or by apps on behalf of) businesspeople.

Technology vendors may provide tools and IT builds systems that span two or more of these theoretically named functions. That makes sense from a software implementation view. However, from a more holistic perspective, it is important to understand the different functions and how they affect data quality and delivery of value to the business.

INSTANTIATION

Instantiation is the process by which measures, events, and messages are represented as instances of data/information within the pillars of the enterprise information space. Mediating information at the boundary of the enterprise, instantiation is the control point for any information that is ingested into the business. Its primary purpose is to ensure that the data/information within the pillars is a valid, useful, usable, and complete representation of the "outer world." It is, therefore, the initial and most important function in driving the generation of high-quality, enterprise data/information.

Approaches to instantiation vary from simple to complex, record- to file-oriented, remote access to transfer and store, push to pull, and real-time to scheduled. These choices depend on the characteristics of the digitally recorded measures, events, and messages from the various sources, as well as on what the business needs from them. Five fundamental forms of instantiation can be identified:

1. **Immediate capture:** Whenever a measure, event, or message of interest is generated on the network, it is noted and recorded within either the MGD or HSI pillar. Ideally, each instance should be recorded once and only once. In some cases, these instances are not stored permanently or, indeed, even for a short time, but are processed on the fly and some summarized version stored for value extraction. The approach is usually implemented in **streaming** tools, and it is commonly seen with high-volume, high velocity, big data sources. Common examples are the capture of telematic data from sensors.

2. **Bulk capture:** Where sources exist as files (or other forms of consolidated data storage, such as databases), bulk capture is the easiest and most obvious means of instantiation. The captured content may consist of measures, events, messages, or even externally generated transactions (not shown in *Figure 4.7*) from a business partner. The rate of change of the data can range from never/seldom—such as the list of states and counties in the US—

to relatively or very frequent—such as daily currency exchange rates or banking transactions.

This type of capture is found in traditional **extract, transform, and load (ETL)** tools—with transform in this case often limited to technical format transformations—as well as simple file-reading programs. As the frequency of change increases, bulk capture becomes less attractive, as the same content is frequently and repeatedly processed, leading to a preference for the next type of instantiation.

3. **Change data capture:** With regularly changing files or other data stores, an initial bulk capture can be followed by regular captures of any changed data, thus minimizing the volume of data being transferred and rewritten. This is usually implemented in **replication** or change data capture tools.

4. **Direct access:** This form of instantiation is used when it is disallowed or technically impractical to copy digitally recorded activities into enterprise-owned storage. Messages from social media sources or documents containing personally identifiable information (PII) are prime sources for direct (programmatic) access to specific information instances.

5. **Transaction generation:** Traditionally, operational systems generate business transactions through data entry and processing. However, in logical terms, operational systems take messages (and, to a lesser extent, events or measures) as input to create transactions. As customers do their own data entry, transactions increasingly originate from browsers, phones, (and even the IoT), and it makes sense to consider all these sources together.

These legally binding transactions, as seen in *"Tri-domain+ model transformations,"* are by far the most significant business information—in operational and informational terms—and require special processing to create completeness and permanence. Transaction generation is thus the most complex and demanding form of instantiation from a data management perspective.

These five modes of instantiation may be embedded in many different (and innocuously named) systems and tools. In addition, an increasing number of implementations—such as **data wrangling**, for example—occur informally, driven by data scientists and others beyond the remit of the IT department. Bulk capture, technically the simplest mode of instantiation, is the most common approach for such informal data acquisition.

Instantiation also uses and stores data/information for its own purposes, for example, temporary datasets, in the information pillars. The diagram does not show this—which would involve overlapping the instantiation block on the foot of the pillars—for ease of reading.

The result of instantiation is that foundational data/information is stored or made available for use within the enterprise. This data/information is understood within a known scope and context, reliance, etc., defined by its associated CSI. In principle, except in the case of transaction generation, such data/information should be as close as possible in form and content to its original source, and, in all cases, any changes made should be fully auditable. As a result, such data/information may or may not be consistent across the pillars; in fact, it is most likely to be at least partially inconsistent. The next two information preparation components ensure the required level of consistency in storage or use.

ASSIMILATION

Assimilation creates derived and reconciled/consistent information sets, using context-setting information in so doing, often across pillars. CSI may also be created by assimilation in this process. Derivation, as the name implies, creates new data/information directly from an already instantiated source, such as translating a code into its full meaning, converting data between measurement units, or using any mathematical summarization functions like sum, mean, etc. Reconciliation and cleansing of data/information apply rules to data/information sets, often from different sources, to ensure quality and consistency.

Two types of inconsistency are recognized. **Semantic inconsistency** arises from differences in definition or structuring of information across source systems. In financial services, customer IDs are notoriously inconsistent because of mergers and acquisitions, where the original systems defined customers differently or used different enumeration schemes. Data modeling and content analysis can determine the rules for reconciling such problems. **Temporal inconsistency** arises when related data/information arrives from two sources at different times and where one dataset may have been updated in the interim. This second type of inconsistency requires more careful and often hand-crafted reconciliation procedures. It is unsupported by most modeling tools and methods, although Anchor modeling (Rönnbäck, 2009), does include some level of temporal support.

In the case of process-mediated data, one important use of assimilation is to support the population of informational systems, such as data warehouses and data marts, from existing transactional data in operational systems that also reside within PMD. Other data/information may also be integrated, if appropriate. Across the information pillars, the most common approach is to create referential links to key values, rather than copying voluminous HSI or MGD into a data warehouse in the PMD pillar, or *vice versa*.

Assimilation is carried out before users have access to the data/information. This pre-planned and pre-executed approach is vital in cases where temporal inconsistency is a feature between different sources. In the past, this has often led to significant delays in making information available, especially in the case of weekly or monthly processing. This is increasingly unacceptable, leading to a drive toward overnight and more frequent updating of source systems. However, some delays are inevitable, particularly in global operations. The point to recognize, however, is that assimilation is specifically aimed at driving a basic level of data/information consistency that can be difficult to achieve in real-time.

These considerations lead to the positioning of the component, as shown in *Figure 4.7*, in close association with CSI, both in using it to drive assimilation and in creating CSI as part of the process.

In technology terms, much of the function of assimilation can be found in the transform part of ETL tooling, but bespoke coding may often be required where source data systems are particularly obscure or arcane. Understanding where and how assimilation is being implemented is of particular importance. Quality gains in the instantiation phase of information preparation can be easily lost through poor understanding or programming in assimilation.

REIFICATION

Reification is the provision of consistent, cross-pillar, **real-time** access to data/information according to an overarching model. It is needed in the pillared information architecture for three distinct reasons:

1. Data/information resides in multiple storage technologies, so a variety of access methods are required to retrieve it and convert it to a common form, often SQL.

2. Where data/information must be joined for specific business needs from these multiple storage technologies, a mediating layer is required to do semantic interpretation and matching, schema translation, and so on.

3. Particularly in the PMD pillar, real-time data/information may not be available in the derived/reconciled informational systems, such as data warehouses or marts. This necessitates real-time joins with the underlying operational systems transactions.

In terms of current technology, the corresponding tools are most often called **data virtualization** or **data federation**; with the exact scope and meaning of these terms differing from vendor to vendor.

With its reliance on an overarching model, reification clearly depends on CSI. In fact, reification and assimilation are also closely interdependent through the CSI they use and generate. Design decisions in assimilation—how customer keys are related, for example—must be echoed and made available in reification to ensure consistency. In addition, as already seen, instantiation and assimilation also display technology overlaps. There is, therefore, a strong argument for a single, integrated set of tooling that addresses all three functional needs, and many vendors cover at least two in their offerings.

Reification may give rise to strong concerns about data quality, due to its real-time delivery of consolidated data/information directly to businesspeople as results of their queries. If mismatches exist in definition or content within the underlying sources, they are likely to *first* be noticed by the business, potentially through incorrect decisions. This contrasts with instantiation and assimilation, where the results of processing are stored in the system *before* the business gets access to them, allowing more opportunity for quality control checks. As a result, data governance should be closely involved in the design of reification function and the models (stored in CSI) by which data and information are joined.

As in the case of instantiation and assimilation, the reification component utilizes the information pillars for its own temporary or intermediated storage purposes and might be more correctly shown as overlapping the tops of the pillars.

From ETL suites to pipelines

Every early data warehousing project had a "before" picture showing a spaghetti-like mess of connections between the operational and informational systems, as well as an "after" picture with a data warehouse being populated via a neat box usually labeled *ETL*. The aim was to replace a plethora of bespoke, individually designed, and largely unmaintainable programs with an integrated, well-understood, and well-managed data population tool.

Extract, transform, and load (ETL) suites of a variety of flavors and breadths have therefore been promoted extensively over the years in traditional data warehousing and, in many cases, have significantly improved the design and maintenance of warehouse population at reduced cost. Of course, such generic solutions can never fully address very specific transformations, so some bespoke coding has always been needed. However, population spaghetti had been largely eliminated in many warehouses by the early 2000s.

Unfortunately, the arrival of big data stores and data lakes reversed this trend. New developers from non-warehousing backgrounds began developing bespoke population code, usually as a "script," specific to each source/target pair all over again. Without ETL tools and lacking in-depth data skills, the result was often incorrect data transformations and the growth of a new "crop" of spaghetti.

As cloud data warehousing has evolved, the term *data pipeline* has become commonplace, and is widely used to describe any and all population approaches. Depending on usage, a data pipeline may connect a data source to a target or may run end-to-end from an initial source all the way to a user app. It typically includes extract, transform, and load function, although additional, more sophisticated function, such as analytics, may be included. The phrase immediately conjures up an image of an individual, one-to-one, bespoke connection from a source to some target. Indeed, much of the current literature on the topic discusses only such one-to-one transfers, emphasizing speed and ease of development, often using no- or low-code approaches.

Some providers of pipeline function may enable the level of integration and reuse seen in ETL suites and, indeed, there is no *a priori* reason why such integration and reuse cannot be included. However, data pipelines, as currently often described, are likely to encourage anew the spread of spaghetti systems to populate the bright and shiny, new cloud data warehouses. A particular concern is in data mesh, where data pipeline design and development is the designated responsibility of the individual data product owners within each business domain, an approach that could easily lead to an explosion of disjoint and disparate data transformations. We return to this topic in Volume II.

SUPPORTING PROCESS FUNCTION

The logical architecture, as shown in *Figure 4.7*, includes three additional components—utilization, administration, and choreography—that surround the information pillars and information preparation functions already discussed.

Utilization

All applications and people's use of information, with their business focus and wide variety of goals and actions, are gathered in the overarching **utilization** component, allowing such business-oriented services to use any and all underlying function and information as required. This is not to suggest a single architected approach to utilization. Rather, this component serves as a placeholder for the many and varied types of tools and methods—BI and analytic tools, AI and machine learning, spreadsheets, and all sorts of data manipulation applications—needed by the business.

There is a temptation, especially with traditional data warehouse pictures showing data flowing only from operational sources to BI tools, to assume a unidirectional information flow "up" the information pillars to utilization. This is not—nor was it ever—valid. Even today, architectural pictures may show only the major data flows to the informational environments, emphasizing the ETL tools and data structures needed to deliver quality, managed data to businesspeople.

However, a "reverse" information flow is also vital in any closed-loop management process. Many people activities do feed information back "down" into the information space. This is most obvious in analytical and planning activities, where models and projected data values are created in BI apps and then become part of the information and CSI in the pillars. Furthermore, people generate all the messages that feed information into the environment, irrespective of whether they order products in web apps or feed the results of analyses back into production systems to tune their behavior. This is shown by the dashed green arrow to the right in *Figure 4.7*. A similar, seldom noticed, reverse arrow was included in the 1988 EBIS architecture shown in *Figure 2.1*.

As we move to cloud data warehousing with its highly distributed architecture, designers of all utilization systems must pay close attention to these "reverse" information flows and their impact on data governance.

Administration

The **administration** component[16] of the logical architecture covers all the design, management, and operational administrative activities relating to both processes and information, as well as to the relationship between people and the underlying spaces. Through this component, information is modeled and managed, services cataloged, application workflows defined and changed, and people's roles and access defined. Some activities, such as security, lie beyond the scope of cloud data warehousing but are, nonetheless, required and expected to exist in the overarching IT architecture.

Administration is usually embedded in specific tools and products at a technology level. However, we depict it here as a single, overarching function because of its key role in creating context-setting information in all areas of the system. It also allows consideration of two other cross-architecture aspects that deserve attention: immediacy and breadth.

Immediacy relates to the fact that a modern business is always changing. Therefore, extra attention must be paid to processes and responsibility for ongoing maintenance of all the CSI produced by administration. We have already seen this in the concept of active metadata in data fabric.

---

[16] Renamed from "Organization" in *Business unIntelligence* for clarity.

A design function such as modeling, for example, can no longer be a task that is done only once: up-front, in advance of implementation. PMD can and must be modeled in advance of its use to ensure valid and consistent structure and contents. On the other hand, a large proportion of HSI, such as emails, must be "modeled" on the fly to determine their meaning. Such modeling, rather than being performed manually, is done in text analytics and ML tools as the information is processed. Modeling will be explored further in Volume II.

Breadth refers to the fact that the boundaries between business and IT are further blurred in cloud data warehousing. Businesspeople create and modify workflows and build complex processes in many analytics activities. IT staff are intimately involved in business design and governance activities where technology is a gating factor. Administration must therefore interact with both business and IT equally, given that it is no longer only IT that can build systems or only business that can define requirements.

The broad scope and diversity of people and organizations involved is thus vast. This dictates that both enterprise architecture and data governance, which span all areas of business and technology, must be engaged in designing a cloud data warehousing environment. And these entities will need to be even more deeply involved if the approach chosen is significantly novel, specifically in the case of data mesh.

Choreography

The final component of the process space, **choreography**[17], provides the framework for a **service-oriented architecture (SOA)** or **microservices** approach that enables workflows to be constructed on the fly from independently defined and built services (well-bounded functional units), as well as a bus architecture that enables them to communicate. Choreography thus coordinates and orchestrates the actions of all participating elements to produce the desired business and/or technical outcomes. It is technically complex and, in many cases, poorly defined or implemented by vendors and internal developers alike.

Nonetheless, it has become mainstream as we move toward cloud data warehousing. The thinking can be seen in data fabric, where it is key to the automation of data management functions, using CSI (there called active metadata) as a foundation. Choreography is at the heart of data mesh, given it is a microservices approach based on modern, cloud-centric software development methodologies.

We will thus return to choreography in more depth as we discuss both data fabric and data mesh in Volume II.

---

[17] Also sometimes called *orchestration*.

TAKEAWAYS

- We identify three data/information domains, based on the characteristics of their structure and management: process-mediated data (PMD), machine-generated data (MGD), and human-sourced information (HSI).

- Context-setting information (CSI)—an extensive and advanced form of metadata—spans all three of the above domains and performs a vital role in describing and contextualizing data/information in its creation and use in the enterprise.

- These three domains form the basic information pillars of the cloud data warehousing logical architecture. These pillars, spanned by CSI to ensure maximum integration, enable data and information to flow most rapidly and with minimum copying from their original sources to their target systems or users.

- In the process space, three main data/information management and access functions—instantiation, assimilation, and reification—represent the core processes of cloud data warehousing.

- They are supported by a set of auxiliary function—utilization, administration, and choreography.

- The logical architecture first defined in *Business unIntelligence* is broadly applicable to on-premises, cloud, and hybrid data warehousing. However, the representation of information pillars is expanded to better represent the multi-location nature of cloud implementations and the ongoing move to use object stores as a preferred data/information management and storage approach in the cloud.

- However, object stores do have limitations in working with regularly changed or updated data. Working around these restrictions at the levels of implementation and technology requires explicitly different thinking in cloud data warehousing.

Chapter 5

BLUE SKIES AND CLOUD ARCHITECTURE

We are called to be architects of the future,
not its victims.

R. Buckminster Fuller

Looking beyond the current view of cloud data warehousing architecture described in Chapters 3 and 4, we may ask where major innovations may be expected. Despite any such innovations that will come, the longevity of the underpinning conceptual and logical architectures just described suggests that changes in the overall appearance of these pictures are likely to be minimal. However, as the old adage goes, the devil is in the detail.

The conceptual level represents the business needs, telling the story: People process information—to make decisions and take action. Although this purpose may seem immutable, the question increasingly arises as to the role of people here. As artificial intelligence becomes pervasive, whither personal responsibility and agency? What of ethics? We turn to the implication of AI and ML in the next section.

At the logical level, technology—both hardware and software—is the main driver of architectural change. This may occur in two places. In the information pillars: What should be stored, where and in what forms? And in the process components: How is all this information created, managed, and accessed? A number of plausible technology advances and directions are of interest here and are the topics of the latter part of this chapter.

IT'S THE AI, STUPID[18]

Perhaps better titled "It's the stupid AI," we focus here on how artificial intelligence may affect cloud data warehousing at the level of the conceptual architecture. Of course, as we shall see later, AI also impinges on the functions and features of the logical architecture, in the areas of both information and process. However, the impact of AI is arguably most significant in the people thinking space, and poses the central questions: In what way will AI affect how decisions are made

---

[18] *Chapeaux* to James Carville's famous "It's the economy, stupid" catchphrase used in Bill Clinton's 1992 presidential campaign.

and how actions are instigated? To what extent will AI displace people as the ultimate driver of decision making and action taking? And, indeed, should it do so?

The consequences of implementing AI are often simply divided into two opposing camps. The first is **automation**. Driven by the need for efficiency and timeliness, automating a process by AI attempts to reduce or eliminate the involvement of people. The second aim, **augmentation**, seeks to improve and enhance people's performance within an existing or improved process. These two aims are often seen as mutually exclusive. In reality, they are two ends of a spectrum, and many AI implementations may contain aspects of both to varying degrees.

In data warehousing, automation of decision making has a long history, dating to the 1990s. Then, simple deterministic logic was applied in operational BI to drive rapid decisions and actions in tasks of relatively limited scope and complexity. AI allows such automation to move to a probabilistic approach and to be applied to a wide range of more ambiguous and complex tasks. AI thus allows automation to move from relatively simple operational decision making to the tactical decision making currently undertaken by administrative staff and middle managers. Examination of many aspects of strategic decision making indicates that parts of these processes may also be amenable to automation. In the tactical case, one may expect some manager roles to be entirely replaced. At the strategic level, automation is more likely to be applied to certain types of activities, rather than wholesale job elimination.

These impacts are likely to be increasingly seen as generative AI (such as OpenAI's ChatGPT) becomes increasingly powerful. Research from Goldman Sachs reports that AI could automate 25% of the entire labor market. However, the impact is highest in administrative jobs (46% of tasks), with high percentages also seen in the legal, architecture, and engineering professions (Jones, 2023). The report claims as "good news … that worker displacement from automation has historically been offset by creation of new jobs." As with many prior studies, this report offers no insights into what these new jobs might be. And it is particularly difficult to see what new jobs might suit displaced managers and decision makers.

In architectural terms, the outcome is a significant reduction in scope and value on all dimensions of the people thinking space. Indeed, the ultimate value of people as decision makers is likely to be meaningfully reduced. This is sometimes justified in terms of reducing human bias or eliminating mistakes. However, when applied to decisions affecting personal welfare and societal good, such automation significantly multiplies the dangers of purely logical/rational thinking—as already discussed in *"The people thinking space"*—by eliminating human ethics or empathy from the process.

The ethics of applying AI in computing and decision making has increasingly exercised thinkers and researchers over the past decade. However, as discussed in *Data Ethics: Practical Strategies for Implementing Ethical Information Management and Governance*, the value or effectiveness of these many efforts is questionable. "Whether by design or as a result of lack of design, organizations fail to translate data ethics principles into actionable policies and outcomes ... [T]here are over 160 distinct frameworks for ethical use of AI or automated decision making, but few of these have any enforcement mechanisms..." (O'Keefe and O Brien, 2023)

In the workplace, AI-driven automation is thus highly likely to be accompanied by job losses among decision makers and middle managers. While often particularly attractive from a financial viewpoint, automation may be seen as socially unacceptable. Augmentation is thus often promoted as preferable, particularly by vendors of AI software and systems. The recent explosion in generative AI—capable of generating hyper-realistic text, images, or other media in response to human prompts—has significantly increased interest in the augmentation of research and decision-making activities. Past experience, however, suggests that the financial benefits of automation—cost reduction—will prove more appealing in most implementation circumstances.

In the context of the people thinking space, augmentation also emphasizes logical/rational thinking. AI augmentation is thus often proposed as a tool to help humans deal with today's explosion of information. It can summarize and abstract "insights" from vast information stores, offer alternative interpretations, and allow the human decision maker to focus on higher-value activity. Allowing the retention of human oversight, augmentation's societal or ethical impact—it is suggested—may be reduced in comparison to automation. However, not only may valid insights be excluded by the AI because of gaps or biases in its information base, but at least in its current state, generative AI is known to "hallucinate," even to the extent of inventing fictitious references to support its conclusions (Moran, 2023).

Whether through automation or augmentation, the result is a reduction in all the dimensions of the people thinking space. The Psychosocial Mindset axis shrinks to little more than logical/rational thinking; the Information Intent axis loses the innovative category, particularly in the case of automation; and Organizational Role reduces to a form of (pseudo-)corporate governance, reflecting the reality that the AI training data is likely to be of sufficient volume and breadth only if it spans the whole organization and beyond.

The outcome, therefore, seems likely to be a reduction in the "human quality" of decision making, a consequence that should cause significant pause for thought. However, the growing belief in the power of AI may cause this to be overlooked. Technochauvinism, a belief that technology is the sole solution to every challenge or opportunity, is a real danger here—as explained in *Artificial Unintelligence: How Computers Misunderstand the World* (Broussard, 2018)—and needs to be guarded against.

The recent, wide-eyed excitement about ChatGPT offers a salutary lesson. Its ongoing, rapid, profit-driven growth—using as its lexicon an undoubtedly biased, flawed, and ultimately un-curated corpus of internet text and imagery—is leading to a massive, unregulated social experiment. It is likely to be used to spread far more disinformation at far greater cost—climate, human, social, and economic—than any good that might come from it. As evidence, we can look at the negative and highly destructive impact of social media, based on similar but far less powerful approaches, in society. This should give an unbiased observer—whether in private or public life, in science or business—significant and lengthy pause for thought.

TECHNOLOGY-DRIVEN EVOLUTION

Setting the above thoughts and concerns aside for now, technological change is also the main driver of evolution at the logical level of data warehousing architecture. Indeed, it was the development of relational database technology and, in particular, IBM's DB2 that set the scene for the first data warehouse architecture in the mid-1980s, as described in *"Enter the data warehouse."* The possibilities offered by evolving technology have long driven data warehousing evolution, from the centralized relational database and SQL of the 1970s to the distributed processing and storage of to-day's cloud systems. It is to emerging changes in storage and database technology that we turn in *"The future of data/in-formation storage."*

THE RISE AND RISE OF AI AND ML

But first, a brief word about AI and ML as they become an integral part of all aspects of data management and pro-cessing in data warehousing. We have already seen their roles in data fabric to create and curate active metadata. Data modeling and data preparation tools are embedding them to automate population processes. BI tools are using them to augment analysis and decision support.

Of particular interest is **decision intelligence**. The term was popularized in *Link: How Decision Intelligence Connects Data, Actions, and Outcomes for a Better World*, (Pratt, 2019) and identified in 2021 by Gartner as a key tech trend. It combines thinking from various domains, such as from social science, decision theory, and managerial science, with data science, especially AI and ML, to enhance organizational decision making. It aims to reduce time and cost in design, development, test, and deployment of complex, "data-driven" decision making. While still very early on the adoption curve, we should look out for further development in decision intelligence, particularly in the use of AI to augment and automate many classes of decision making.

THE FUTURE OF DATA/INFORMATION STORAGE

The one significant transformation in the 2013 logical architecture has already been shown in the change between *Figure 4.4* and *Figure 4.6*—the merging of the information pillars at their foot, driven by the adoption of cloud-based object stores as a base for data storage. This reflects a shift in technological possibilities and might cause us to ask if we are heading toward a single storage or database solution (or perhaps far fewer than currently in use) capable of handling all types of data equally, and leading architecturally to the merging of the pillars over their entire height.

Object stores and beyond

Cloud-based object stores will continue to evolve from their write-once, read-many, "unstructured" big data origins. Cloud data warehousing is strongly driving their use toward the more highly structured process-mediated data (PMD) that comes from operational systems and machine-generated data (MGD) from the IoT. Such use is likely to enable data to be treated at an increasingly granular level, allowing traditional insert, update, and delete operations to be optimally performed. Thus, we already see "transactional tables" being built on this base, a direction that is being strongly adopted in the data lakehouse. Open-source table formats, such as Delta Lake, Apache Iceberg, and Apache Hudi, with inbuilt record-level operations, built on top of object stores, are thus likely to see significant further adoption by cloud data warehousing vendors, driven by growing market acceptance of the data lakehouse approach.

In the longer term, the traditional distinction between operational and informational systems—dating back to (and before) the earliest days of on-premises data warehousing—is likely to become less clear in the cloud environment. Data entry on smartphones and websites by consumers and internal users of an organization generates process-mediated data (PMD) in the same cloud environments where data warehousing is implemented. This allows developers to consider building combined operational/informational systems.

Similar moves have been considered in traditional on-premises data warehouses over the past decade or more, driven by business needs for more timely data and conjoined operational/informational applications. This has been most successfully delivered in SAP HANA (High-performance ANalytic Appliance), a proprietary approach using a multi-model, in-memory database that supports advanced analytics and high-speed transactions in a single system.

Cloud database and cloud data warehouse vendors may therefore consider whether faster, cheaper compute and the shift of persistent data storage from hard disk to memory might together enable a reduction in specialized storage structures and types of databases and stores. Set against this, however, must be the continuing growth in data storage volumes and business requirements for ever more timely access. In addition, different data structures offer more than performance gains; they fundamentally enable more appropriate models for thinking about and implementing solutions for differing types of data/information, as well as its interrelationships and meaning.

This debate is likely to continue, and we might see some of the more esoteric data stores fall out of favor. Relational databases will, however, certainly persist and improve and will remain the workhorse of most cloud data warehousing needs. Another structure, graphs, to which we next turn, will become increasingly important.

Graph databases

Following nearly a decade when NoSQL was declared as the answer to all data ills, relational database technology has reemerged as the primary vehicle for delivery of data warehousing in general and in the cloud. This revival is due in part to the underpinning mathematical basis of the relational model, first defined by Dr. E.F. Codd (Codd, 1970) and further extended over subsequent decades by Chris Date (Date, 2004). Add to this the relative simplicity of the SQL language and its popularity with IT and business alike (Chamberlin and Boyce, 1974) and (Chamberlin, 2012).

However, the relational model is not the answer in all cases either. Oddly, and despite the name, the relational model has nothing to do with *relationships* in the everyday use of the word. For such relationships, you need graph databases (or a high EQ, emotional quotient!). And it is the graph model that provides a very different and valuable way of looking at data and information.

There are two broad classes of graph database—labeled property graphs (LPGs) and resource description framework

(RDF) triple stores—each with its own characteristics and strengths. In both cases, the world is described in terms of nodes and edges. Nodes represent things of interest and edges are the relationships between them. *Figure 5.1* shows a simple Wikipedia example of a labeled property graph.

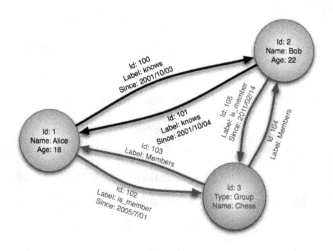

Figure 5.1: Labeled property graph[19]

The nodes represent two people and a chess group of which they are members. The edges show the relationships between them—knowing one another or being members of the chess group. In an LPG, each node and edge is labeled with properties, such as names, descriptors, values, creation

---

[19] Source: Wikipedia user Achim Friedland, Creative Commons CC0 1.0, commons.wikimedia.org/wiki/File:GraphDatabase_PropertyGraph.png.

or modification dates, etc., often represented as key : value pairs in JSON. This approach is both user-friendly and particularly useful for applications that involve following relationship links, such as recommendation systems and in social media networks.

While LPGs are more easily understood, and often more performant, RDF triple stores are more formal and the basis of knowledge graphs, as we shall see in the following section. RDF is based on simple logical assertions of the form **subject → predicate → object triples**, such as "Bob is 35" or "Mary knows Bob." As explained in "Graph Fundamentals" (Feeney, 2019), **"triples are the ideal atom of information**—3 degrees of freedom in our basic atomic expressions is sufficient for a self-describing system... We can build up a set of triples that describes anything describable. Binary relations, on the other hand, which are the basis of tables and traditional databases, can never be self-describing: they will always need some logic external to the system to interpret them."

In RDF, nodes and edges are URIs (Uniform Resource Identifiers) and often link to self-describing ontologies. This leads to a verbose notation but doesn't assume any prior knowledge of the meanings of any terms used. It is this characteristic that is particularly attractive for a cloud data warehousing environment where the volume and variety of data is so large that manually defining and maintaining separate knowledge of meanings is well-nigh impossible.

WHAT IS THIS THING CALLED *PROFIT*?

Profit, Customer Address, Price, and a host of similar words and phrases form the core of business discourse. But probe a little deeper or put colleagues from different departments in the same meeting and you quickly discover that different words mean the same thing (synonyms), the same words mean different things (polysemes), and one apparently identical thing has three different formulae for calculating it, one of which is outdated but still used in one system (a bug or a feature?!).

A word of warning. This topic has been well hyped many times in the history of data warehousing, and with limited success in delivering solutions. Yes, we must discuss data catalogs, knowledge graphs, and so-called "business metadata". Unfortunate history or not, solving the issue of meaning will be central to cloud data warehousing.

In *"One last time: data vs. information,"* we discussed how and why it is important to distinguish between these two concepts and the role that context plays in doing so. We also observed how the words may be used interchangeably and often incorrectly in common discourse. Similar concerns apply to *knowledge* and *meaning,* as we will discuss in depth in

Volume II. However, for the businesspeople and others who use the output of data warehousing, knowing and agreeing (as needed) the meaning of what is being discussed or delivered is vital.

This need has become overwhelming in the distributed and diverse world of cloud data warehousing. We are promised increased democratization of data distributed throughout the enterprise, courtesy of the cloud. But given that it is information that business truly needs, it is to the meanings and interrelationships—context-setting information (CSI)—contained within that information that we must next turn.

And the question that must be answered is: Why might we be more likely to succeed now, given past struggles to deliver metadata even in a simpler, less distributed world? Recognizing full well that technology is only part of any solution, those currently emerging must seek to overcome prior barriers to success, both human and technical.

Knowledge graphs and a semantic layer

This technology evolution is seen specifically in new approaches to the storage and use of context-setting information / metadata in specific types of databases, such as knowledge graphs. Meanwhile, in the people space, the collection and moderation of CSI is being improved by machine learning. Such progress is too low level to appear in the logical architecture shown in *Figure 4.6*, rather we see it in technology advances and product developments. Indeed, much of this is foreshadowed in the data fabric and data mesh approaches already introduced.

The previous section introduced RDF triple stores and noted their self-describing nature. Such self-description is a key characteristic in future information modeling and context-setting information systems, and is the foundation of knowledge graphs. We have already seen this in the connected knowledge graph defined in data fabric (see *"Weaving a data fabric"*). Related to this is the concept of a **semantic layer**—in essence, an access layer that allows businesspeople to find and use diverse data mediated by a knowledge graph that translates business terminology and meaning to IT database and column names, location, access methods, etc.

A knowledge graph therefore stands at the heart of all aspects of the relationship between data as stored in cloud data warehousing and the information that is its defining source. A knowledge graph thus defines data meanings, its sources and ultimate uses, and how they all relate. Both that definition and subsequent usage in all circumstances originates with the business and its people. A knowledge graph, supplemented with machine learning techniques in its population and construction, thus offers an excellent store for all aspects of CSI and provides the means of exploring the relationships between them (Sequeda, 2022).

These considerations lead directly to the need to apply novel thinking to the entire area of data (or, better, information) modeling, which today is a central pillar in the creation of CSI. As explained in *Graph Data Modeling for NoSQL and SQL* (Frisendal, 2016), the original exposition of entity-relationship (ER) modeling (Chen, 1976) was conceived as business-facing or conceptual in scope. However, as the technique was adopted as the basis for relational database design, more technical concerns were embedded. According to Frisendal, "The attributes were folded into the entities, which became tables. The diagrams began to fill with little icons, giving them a distinctly engineering flavor. At this point, conceptual models almost completely disappeared; most analyses started at the 'logical' data model [idealized data structure] level."

The need to return to business-oriented information modeling (as opposed to IT-driven data modeling) has never been more urgent, and the methods and tools are now emerging. There is an appetite to address the problems and opportunities as cloud data warehousing becomes pervasive. And I believe there is finally a chance to succeed. We will explore these topics further in Volume II when we dive deeper into data fabric and data mesh. However, the takeaway for now is that knowledge graphs offer a foundation for the automation of data management in building, operating, and using cloud data warehousing.

The need for an "information context management system"

Returning to relational databases, we know from Chapter 3 that the data tables contain naked data, while the context (or metadata)—table names, column names, and (if the DBAs do a good job) table and column descriptions, etc.—is stored separately in system tables. Most relational databases are designed in third normal form or some derivative of that, such that user tables generally represent business entities or the relationships between them, with the relevant context stored in the system tables. This design approach is what leads to the ease of use of relational databases by business-people (subject to the *caveats* in the previous section).

However, it should be noted that the context stored—and the design of the data tables themselves—is actually the *creation context*, as we saw in *"One last time: data vs. information."* And it is likely that many usage contexts exist in addition. The challenge is that a relational database can only store one set of context information at a time: typically, the creation context. As a result, in cloud data warehousing, we must build and populate a second database to hold the context (as well as the data, of course) needed for analytical tasks. In fact, we may end up building multiple databases for many different usage contexts.

A similar problem arises in the onboarding and use of externally sourced data. Such external information is often largely decontextualized (for example, in CSV format files) as it is passed over the internet to the receiving enterprise. **Data wrangling** (a common term, along with data munging, in the data science community to describe *ad hoc* data preparation) is, in effect, the rebuilding of the context needed to interpret and use the incoming data. But, once again, only one such context can be stored in a traditional database.

The underlying problem is the same: We need multiple usage contexts for the same base data set. The database creator embeds the CSI for their original usage scenario in the database design. Subsequent usage scenarios pose varying levels of mismatch to that original design. As usage scenarios become ever more varied and complex, we need something beyond a traditional database to manage the mix and match of uses of the data it contains. This suggests that beyond databases to store data that can be used in multiple contexts, we need some form of "information context management system" that allows multiple contexts for the same set of data to be stored and managed, which are then the basis for using the same underlying data in multiple, different contexts.

This preliminary thinking is based on an analysis[20] of a novel database structure, used in a system called CortexDB. This is based on a combination of a document store that holds the naked data and an integrated set of sixth normal form (6NF) indexes that stores the context. The approach could form the basis for a more comprehensive treatment of data and information and their interrelationship in future data warehousing systems. 6NF is also at the heart of the graph normal form (GNF) promoted by RelationalAI to allow flexibility and scalability in building and querying enterprise-scale knowledge graphs (Herskovitz, 2021).

Context in code

Before closing on the topic of context, we must visit one final canyon of chaos. It's a place where knowledge graphs and ontologies are of less help: the context widely encoded in the Python and Java code created by programmers to populate and maintain all flavors of data warehousing solutions.

Consider "Profit" one last time. We may define its meanings in different departments and over various timespans in CSI, ontologies, and knowledge graphs. Such definitions will be of significant value to businesspeople who need to know

---

[20] Further details can be found in "CortexDB Reinvents the Database" (Devlin, 2019).

which variety of "profit" we are discussing. However, we must not forget the process space—the code that was written to calculate the different values.

Ideally, the code implements what is represented in the CSI, all of what's there, and only what's there. In reality, such code has, to some extent, a life of its own. Some aspects of calculating profit are more easily done in code than in the logical model. Even in cases where the transformation was first modeled, system maintenance and upgrades may neglect to update the model in the urgency to fix the code. Novice programmers make mistakes; old programmers die. There are many ways in which context becomes entombed in code and creates growing technical debt.

We may envisage AI systems that can disentangle such encoded context and restore it to its rightful place in the models, ontologies, and knowledge graphs of the enterprise. I am unaware of any efforts to address this at present.

TAKEAWAYS

- AI is certain to become (an even bigger) part of cloud data warehousing. In the people space, its impact at the ethical and societal levels will demand careful consideration and strong regulation, particularly by organizations that have direct financial or civil impacts on people, both internal and external to the business.

- As separate (as well as co-located) storage and computing technology evolves and improves in the cloud environment, the debate will intensify about differing storage formats and database structures for different business needs and data/information domains. There exists a strong urge toward "a single copy of data" for all operational, reporting, and analytic purposes. However, only limited progress in this direction is likely in the near future.

- A key area of evolution is likely to involve the broad area of context-setting information (CSI), in its collection, structure, and storage in a highly distributed cloud world, its uses in all aspects of information creation and use, for automation of governance and management, and for operation and maintenance of cloud data warehousing solutions. Success in this area will be vital for the future of cloud data warehousing.

- These technology-led developments are foreshadowed strongly in the emerging data fabric and data mesh approaches.

Chapter 6

The Journey to Cloud Data Warehousing

We don't receive wisdom; we must discover it for ourselves
after a journey that no one can take for us or spare us.

Marcel Proust

Every journey begins from the same place: from wherever we find ourselves today. In IT, whatever the strengths or weaknesses of our current solution, that is where we start. Irrespective of whether the new business needs are the same as those for which we developed the existing solution or a major change to or extension of them. When it comes to data warehousing, most modern cloud solutions start from on-premises systems that date back many years; green-field sites are seldom, if ever, found anymore.

Furthermore, we start with a set of knowledge of and skills in technology and methodology; and, indeed, preferences that drive choices and behaviors, often unconsciously. Sometimes those preferences differ wildly from our existing skills, especially when new management arrives with gems of wisdom gleaned from the popular IT press, the glossy marketing materials of hungry vendors, or expensive MBA programs. In such cases, *caveat emptor*, or perhaps more appropriately, implementer beware.

In all cases, we should learn from the prior experience of real data warehousing veterans. Although there is much new technology and many novel methods underpinning cloud data warehousing, it should be clear from the preceding architectural discussion that much of that derives directly from the broader field of data warehousing as it has evolved over nearly four decades.

And on this common foundation, we can observe that most cloud data warehousing implementation journeys begin principally from one of three existing states:

1. An existing on-premises "data warehouse classic" of one of the flavors described earlier in *"Competing data warehouse structures."*

2. An existing "data lake classic", either on-premises or in the cloud as seen in *"But... what is a data lake?"*

3. Ongoing cloud uptake, driven either by operational app delivery, often with siloed reporting approaches,

or by large-scale analytical or AI/ML systems—cloud-based data lakes.

The adverb *principally* above serves to remind us that the first data warehouse classic state may often coexist with one or both of the other two. This is because many enterprises have existing data warehouses that were developed to support reporting and BI needs and continue to do so, even while new, bright and shiny, mostly analytic, needs are being delivered through paths 2 and/or 3 above. Nonetheless, it still makes sense to consider them separately, as is done in the following sections.

First, however, we should introduce the concept of architectural design patterns (ADPs).

NOW, ARCHITECTURAL DESIGN PATTERNS

There exists on the internet and elsewhere a plethora of definitions and pseudo-definitions of data warehousing-related terms. We have seen some already, such as data lake and lakehouse, data mesh and data fabric. Some have been offered by thought leaders and experts in the field, often with experience in delivering working solutions. Some come from vendors, often based on what their current product sets deliver. All reflect an understanding based at a point in time, in rapidly evolving business and technology environments.

Many use the same terms to describe subtly or distinctly different things. In other cases, the same solution is named as two different things. Indeed, some solutions are described as a combination of different things, such as, a vendor may suggest that their offering applies "data mesh concepts" on top of a "data fabric base" to deliver a "data lakehouse solution." I exaggerate only a little. But what could this possibly mean?

Such a definition (or pseudo-definition) is, at best, marketing fluff or, at worst, patent nonsense. A phrase such as *data xxx* should be capable of a single definition that we agree to use for the purposes of discussion and comparison.

To this end, I offer the **architectural design pattern (ADP)**. Its purpose is to offer a set of terminology and, usually, a picture[21], on which we can agree, at least throughout our current discussion. An ADP thus encapsulates the key business needs and fundamental infrastructure requirements and constraints of a particular solution approach. In this sense, therefore, data warehouse classic, logical data warehouse, and data lake are the three foundational patterns that underpin almost all current thinking about analytics and decision-making support (and their relationship to transaction

---

[21] Volume II will unveil the pictures for the newer ADPs, as well as the current foundational patterns. ☺

processing in operational systems). Data lakehouse, data fabric, and data mesh are also ADPs. The following definitions underpin all the implementation thinking in this chapter, as well as provide a foundation for the discussions in Volume II:

- **Data warehouse classic (DWC):** provides correct and consistent, well-modeled, schema-on-write, relevant, and usable information in support of business analysis and decision-making needs in a cross-business manner. To each adjective above, we may add: *as far as possible*. A DWC may be structured as a hub-and-spoke pattern consisting of an enterprise data warehouse (EDW) and dependent data marts, as a dimensional / star-schema pattern, or some combination of both.

  As we've already seen, there is minimal difference between on-premises and cloud at the level of the logical architecture. However, technology can and does drive important differences at the physical implementation level. We, therefore, distinguish between two flavors of this ADP when necessary:

  o **DWC/op:** implemented with technologies traditionally used **on-premises**, based on finite servers or server clusters, using "conventional" relational database technologies from vendors such as IBM, Oracle, or Teradata.

On-premises here refers to the technology rather than physical location. A data warehouse based on this technology can be lift-and-shifted to the cloud (essentially a move to infrastructure-as-a-service).

o **DWC/cn**: built on **cloud-native** technology, which is loosely defined[22] as automatically elastic and scalable, leveraging object storage, with clearly separate compute and storage, and multi-cluster compute.

• **Logical data warehouse (LDW)**: extends a DWC with direct, real-time access to data in other sources, such as operational systems, files, NoSQL stores, etc. Access is mediated through an overarching logical data model describing the different data sources in a common language. It also insulates users from underlying differences in format and meaning. Businesspeople typically access all the data through SQL or SQL-based apps. The LDW decomposes and transforms SQL to whatever interface

---

[22] Another useful approach to framing *cloud native* uses LIFESPAR: Latency-aware, Instrumented, Failure-aware, Event-driven, Secure, Parallelizable, Automated, and Resource consumption-aware. See *"Making sure it works in the cloud"* for details.

is required by the individual sources and returns a joined result to the user using data virtualization technology.

- **Data lake classic (DLC):** offers data in raw, as-received format, usually with limited preprocessing, or with cleansing at the discretion of the business user. Key characteristics include scalable data storage in any format, multiple processing models, and timely, flexible usage (schema-on-read) by businesspeople. In many cases, data governance is limited, leading to multiple, overlapping, and inconsistent "copies" (exact or otherwise) of the same data being stored, and users left to their own devices to figure out which data to use when.

- **Data lakehouse:** proposes an elastic cloud solution to a combination of DWC and DLC needs, despite their clearly conflicting nature. It offers an environment based on an object store as a single well-governed storage layer for all structured and semi-structured data, managed and accessed through relational-like function, either via a database or Spark (or similar function), and governed through technical metadata support. In addition, loosely structured (so-called "unstructured") data is included, as found in DLC.

As we shall see more clearly in Volume II, the data lake-house ADC differs only marginally in semantics and initial focus from the DWC/cn pattern defined above.

- **Data fabric:** essentially an extension of the LDW patern, offers enhanced management and automation of data storage, population, access, and all aspects of data management in a diverse, distributed environment usually centered on a DWC in either of its flavors. This is supported via AI-enhanced and -extended active metadata that reflects the real, changing, live business and computing environment across the entire set of data stores and processes.

- **Data mesh:** proposes a highly distributed, analytics-focused environment that shuns conventional approaches to centralizing data in warehouses or lakes (to ensure flexibility and agility in development and delivery), and instead promotes domain-driven design to deliver data as a product. Such data products are realized and managed by combined business/IT teams within business domains, with a focus on embedded, distributed governance and infrastructure-as-a-platform. The technological implementation of many of these concepts is currently less well-defined and open to interpretation by designers, vendors, and implementers. (And they do.)

STARTING POINT: EXISTING ON-PREMISES DWC

As already seen, the data warehouse classic ADP majors on delivering high-quality data—or, better, information. By *high quality*, we mean well-defined, reconciled across the enterprise, and error-free. Approaches to supporting this goal include data modeling into predefined relational database schemas, layering of data, and the use of metadata to describe the environment. The main problem is that data warehouses are often slow to build and challenging to maintain as business needs evolve and data sources change. In addition, the delivery of information to businesspeople may be slower than they desire, especially where extensive layering is present.

Twentieth-century DWC builders fought hard to overcome these issues. But, in many cases, lower-quality workarounds were adopted by departmental IT groups at the behest of businesspeople desperate for quick results. These workarounds include departmental "data warehouses" and directly sourced (independent) data marts. Since the early 2000s, externally sourced big data has exacerbated these challenges. A growing business need for extreme data timeliness, as well as the cost-motivated drive to move the relational base of the warehouse first to Hadoop and then to cloud technologies, have only made the situation worse.

Sometimes described by the early 2020s as a "data mess," cloud data warehousing implementers starting from here are therefore faced with a technologically complex, largely on-premises environment for data provision. Where a logical data warehouse or data lake (perhaps in the cloud) has been added, the outcome is wildly varying levels of data quality across multiple environments. Although often largely insulated from the data lake, and with the cloud on the horizon, these prospective cloud data warehousing implementers stand on the shores of the Island of Information shown in *Figure 2.3*, watching the data lake waters rising around them and wondering both how to maintain quality and react to the changing technology landscape with appropriate speed and flexibility.

MIGRATION FROM THE DWC

Perhaps the most important, over-arching principle in data warehousing implementation is to avoid a multi-year, "big bang" project and instead take a series of small, business-related steps toward the final goal. This approach was defined as far back as the mid-1990s in *Data Warehouse: from Architecture to Implementation* (Devlin, 1997) and can be equally and fruitfully applied to a migration from a DWC/op to a data warehousing solution in the cloud.

STAGED CLOUD DATA WAREHOUSING IMPLEMENTATION

Figure 6.1 below shows a staged cloud data warehousing implementation program consisting of a number of projects that deliver cloud-based function, as well as on-premises retirement projects, all defined in a staged implementation roadmap (SIR).

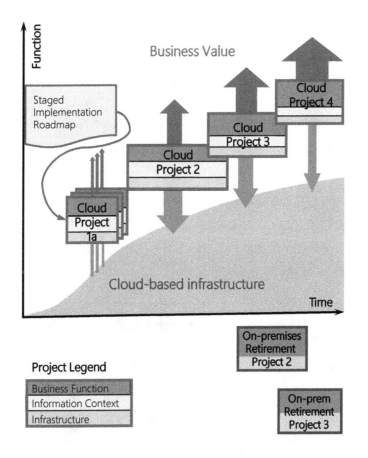

Figure 6.1 The staged implementation program and roadmap

As we progress through the program, each cloud project delivers increasing business function and value, and decreasing increments of infrastructure, both occurring over shorter time spans and with less resources. In the case of information context delivery (or modeling), the graphic shows this occurring and also decreasing with time. However, if the modeling has been largely done in the DWC/op era and remains valid for the business, we may expect this work to be minimal or, at least, less daunting in the cloud migration. On-premises retirement projects occur, as one might expect, when the corresponding cloud project has been delivered.

The staged implementation roadmap, SIR, provides an overarching plan for the *program*. Unlike a project plan, the SIR has no commitments to either specific deliverables or schedule, with one important exception noted below. It must be signed off by C-level executives across the business organization and (importantly) IT in terms of its overall approach. It confirms agreement to the broad approach and timescale with specific decisions, as well as checkpoints where such decisions are made and may be changed.

If successful, the SIR will convince management that the cloud migration is essential, achievable, and will gain their support for its implementation. To some extent, the SIR is an internal marketing brochure that provides a vision of the migration and an assurance that it can be done. Unlike many documents produced by the IT organization, style and production issues such as layout, readability, use of color, understandable diagrams, etc., are important. In general, it should be less than 50 pages long, and a senior manager should be able and *want* to read it over a glass or two of wine or orange juice!

Furthermore, the SIR is conceived as a living document that will evolve and change over time. Its key components are a strategy review, an outline of the existing situation, high-level architectural views, potential benefits and costs, implications for new and existing systems, a proposed organizational structure (especially a team to manage the evolution of the SIR), a view of project deliverables over time, and—the one area of firm commitment—the scope, deliverables, and timeframe for cloud Projects 1a (and 1b and 1c as needed) and 2 shown in Figure 6.1.

Worth considering in Project 1a is the introduction of data virtualization technology as a layer between all utilization (user apps) and the existing warehouse, marts, and other stores if present. This allows the migration of parts of the existing environment to the new platform largely invisibly to the businesspeople using the data.

Making sure it works in the cloud

This last area is the key difference between the SIR for a traditional DWC and the cloud migration SIR. Project 1a (and 1b and 1c) are essential proofs-of-concept in the cloud environment. These are deemed necessary in the still relatively immature cloud data warehousing environment, particularly because:

1. The database technology, especially where based on an object store, is likely to have very different performance characteristics than a more mature on-premises database. In cases where moving to the cloud involves a change of underlying database product, especially from different vendors, it is highly unlikely that the clever SQL functionality and tools that were used on-premises will even exist or be exactly replicable in the cloud database.

   And while the target vendor may well provide wizards or even free support for the migration, some parts of the query base will likely require manual rewrites. Only where the database vendor explicitly confirms compatibility between the on-premises and cloud database versions can you rest easy on this front.

2. The population processes for a cloud-based data warehouse are significantly different and likely more complex than those in the prior on-premises implementation.

If you have written this function in the warehouse database (often called **extract, load, and transform, ELT**), the exact same concerns as for queries arise, but likely more intractable, given the procedural, complex, and highly specific nature of such code.

If you were using common population (ETL) products, migration to newer versions or different products might be needed to gain cloud and hybrid functionality.

The LIFESPAR principles, defined by Gartner, provide a useful framework for all cloud implementations (Tiwari, 2023), and can be directly applied to cloud data warehousing:

- *Latency-aware:* the ability to deal well with delays in response time.

- *Instrumented:* generate and gather data about usage, to support elastic, automatic scaling.

- *Failure-aware:* able to wait or fail over and recover as needed.

- *Event-driven:* the use of events for communication to simplify scaling and increase resilience.

- *Secure:* to inevitable malicious activity.

- *Parallelizable:* scaling out rather than scaling up, with small, independently scalable components.

- *Automated:* for efficiency and robust disaster recovery.

- ***Resource-consumption-aware:*** despite almost limitless processing and storage, designed to use the minimum cloud resources possible.

The bottom line: unless you are migrating an on-premises data warehouse to an equivalent warehouse and tooling from the same vendor(s)[23], you must make contingency plans for significant effort and unexpected costs.

These significant risks are why the first projects in *Figure 6.1* are limited in scope, and they are more likely to focus on new business needs that can be prototyped and delivered without fear of compromising existing warehousing commitments. Therefore, Project 2 is the first full-scale, business-critical cloud data warehouse project.

STARTING POINT: EXISTING ON-PREMISES OR CLOUD DLC

In contrast to the DWC pattern, data lake classic (DLC) tends to place a very high value on technology—often open-source and increasingly cloud—above all else. In many cases,

---

[23] This approach, called *lift-and-shift,* offers a fast and relatively painless migration to the cloud but does not take advantage of the technological cloud-native strengths and may lead to later rework to address data quality, cost of unused data, etc.

data lake developers' backgrounds are more aligned with application development than the data management and administrator experience of many classic data warehouse implementers. This may lead to a reduced understanding of data quality issues and a reduced ability to design and deliver data-centric solutions.

As described in *"When lakes became swamps,"* these data quality issues are a result of differing, unintegrated data stores, a lack of data management and metadata, and the adoption of a schema-on-read philosophy. Such warnings of "data swamps" have been borne out in many instances. In parallel, many organizations were driven to the new technology due to financial and/or political considerations. Unfortunately, the technology was often too immature to support data warehousing principles. And politics is often a poor basis for technical decisions. As a result, the DLC is left struggling without any visible means of meeting the two partially incompatible drivers we regularly meet: consistency and timeliness.

More recently, this ADP has faced the challenge of streaming data from both internal and external sources, and a growing demand to support both informational and quasi-operational needs. This adds further to the consistency vs. timeliness challenge and has driven the emergence of the data lakehouse ADP. As we've seen, this replaces NoSQL stores with a solution based on the relational paradigm. The Island of Information in *Figure 2.3* is encroaching into the Lake of Data! The old, tried and tested approaches of schema-on-read, a variety of non-relational data stores, and extensive bespoke development are being challenged. This is leading to an almost existential crisis of how to structure data within the lake for the combination of high-speed operational function and complex informational analytics needed by the modern business.

MIGRATION FROM THE DLC

Many data lake owners have accepted that the traditional data lake classic ADP is a dead end and have already begun the search for new approaches. The first step was typically to expand metadata management support with novel tooling and new organizational processes. However, this can only take you so far.

The second and arguably most important step is seen in the move toward supporting more warehouse-like function, culminating in a move to a data lakehouse.

As described in the original article (Lorica, et al., 2020), the goal of a lakehouse is to combine the "best elements of data lakes and data warehouses." In simple terms, this means that the key focus of this ADP is to offer data structures that closely resemble those of data warehouses, with their emphasis on schema-on-write rather than the schema-on-read thinking of the data lake. Although the original free-flowing precepts of data lake remain part of the data lakehouse ADP, they are largely downplayed in favor of these warehouse-like principles.

In fact, data lakehouse formalizes a trend that had already been occurring as lakes began to move to the cloud in the late 2010s. This period saw the (largely externally sourced) data in the lakes become ever more integrated with operational processes in the business, and more internally sourced PMD routed through (or into) the data lake. Consequently, the need to move toward the level of data management and governance seen in a data warehouse—in essence, the adoption of data warehouse fundamentals—has grown. It is thus clear that the first step to the cloud for an organization using the DLC pattern is the formal, technical integration of a data warehouse into the lake or the adoption of a data lakehouse approach. In many cases, the former of these approaches has already been taken and the latter is under consideration.

Perhaps the biggest area of distinction between the data lakehouse and the data warehouse classic ADPs is in their data sourcing strategies. Traditionally, the DWC/op—for a variety of historical technical reasons—tended to favor batch orientation in data preparation. This strongly supports the data consistency aim of the warehouse. As the business demand for data timeliness has increased, batch feeds have moved to shorter intervals, and have often been supplemented by change capture techniques.

Data lakes and lakehouses, because of their early focus on fast-flowing, externally sourced data, have tended to implement streaming tools and systems for the initial population, although later stages of transformation may remain batch based. (This should not be surprising; such transformation stages often demand the combining of data from different sources, and addressing temporal inconsistency issues may be challenging.) Information preparation is thus an aspect of cloud data warehousing that is still undergoing significant evolution. However, lessons learned from decades of data warehouse implementation will remain central for moving from a data lake to cloud data warehousing, represented here by the data lakehouse ADP.

DLC implementers are likely to be more familiar than their DWC peers with object stores and other cloud / open-source stores and tools. Therefore, the migration from traditional on-premises technology may be less of an issue. Nonetheless, adopting a staged cloud implementation plan, as in the previous case, would be good practice, as it is in all warehouse implementations.

LAKE TO LAKEHOUSE OR LAKE TO WAREHOUSE?

Given the limited architectural difference between the DWC/cn and data lakehouse ADPs already mentioned, we may well ask if an existing data lake implementation should migrate to one or the other. In truth, the choice is more a matter of nomenclature than of architecture! The central focus of both ADPs is on delivering consistent, timely, schema-on-write data to the business.

Data lakehouse emphasizes, in addition, the relationship of this warehouse-like data to the less structured and lower quality lake-like data. However, their actual integration, so far, is architecturally and technically rather weak in practice. Data lakehouse further puts more emphasis on streaming as a population method than DWC, either on-premises or in the cloud. However, at a detailed level, there are many technical and methodological overlaps. Both data lakehouse and DWC/cn rely on object store, elastic processing and storage, separation of compute and storage, and multi-cluster technologies. Both require and use modeling and metadata in similar ways.

The bottom line, therefore, may be more about what it's politically expedient to name your new, bright and shiny, cloud environment. Indeed, similar reasoning about naming may apply in projects migrating from an on-premises DWC to the cloud, as described in "*Migration from the DWC.*"

STARTING POINT: ONGOING CLOUD UPTAKE

In many organizations, the ongoing and accelerating move of operational apps and advanced analytics to the cloud—especially during the past decade—is first and foremost driven by technology considerations and aspirations. The belief—on occasion true—is that modern technology surpasses previous generations in abilities, performance, and more. This position is often supported by a financial outlook that favors OpEx (operational expenditure) over CapEx (capital expenditure) in many organizations. At present, there is little appetite among business or IT to debate these underlying financial assumptions.

In addition, the cloud is the undisputed, natural home for modern analytical applications because of their AI-based nature and largely external data sourcing. Traditional reporting and BI for cloud-based operational apps most logically sit with them in the cloud, driving the urge to try to move current on-premises BI and reporting to the cloud in tandem.

The migration of operational function and BI to the cloud and the deployment of analytical function there will therefore continue apace. However, the outsourcing of in-depth technical skills and knowledge that may often accompany cloud implementation may conceal the real, added complexity of data management in the cloud.

None of this cloudy thinking, in essence, changes the underlying components of the *mappa mundi* shown in *Figure 2.3*. However, it does drive significant reconsideration of the consequences of highly distributed cloud data—often together with on-premises data—and especially its governance and management.

The very word *cloud* implies that data locality can be ignored. Users may certainly expect to. IT may be tempted to do so as well. However, from an implementer's point of view, cloud data resides very much on the ground, in various real geographic locations, and with various levels of technically driven caching applied. This may be less important for operational apps with well-bounded functionality and data scopes. However, keep in mind the data sizes seen in lakes and warehouses, the common need to integrate and join data across disparate sources, and the high-speed access often needed in data warehousing. As a result, physical location becomes a vital consideration in everything from cross-border legal concerns to query performance, information preparation, and delivery of results to users. Add multicloud and hybrid on-premises/cloud implementations, and the governance complexity expands dramatically.

Cloud implementers of operational apps may often lack experience with data in breadth and depth. Data management and database administration approaches for a well-bounded dataset of a few dozen fields seldom work for the highly interrelated, complex, thousand-field schemas of the warehousing world. Procedures that are simple and cheap for a few megabytes or gigabytes of data grow rapidly and perhaps exponentially in complexity and cost at the terabyte and petabyte scale. App-level data management and governance techniques seldom scale well to the warehouse or lake environments.

Upgrading existing cloud environments

The key considerations in upgrading existing cloud environments to cloud data warehousing, therefore, revolve around addressing distributed data management concerns, both in terms of data storage and population processes. These may differ depending on whether the migration is coming from a cloud environment designed for largely operational activities (perhaps with simple, single-app operational reporting and BI) or from one that is focused on big data analytics and AI.

Upgrading existing analytics in the cloud

The cloud, with its elastic nature and cost-effective storage and processing is the natural location for analytics—especially that relating to externally sourced big data—and from there to the innovations of AI and ML. In all meaningful respects, this is a modern, cloud-based data lake classic ADP. The requirement is mainly for raw or lightly processed data, often in wide-record, loosely structured, or non-relational formats from many independent and often unplanned sources; and for its extensive exploratory and iterative processing. This is pure data science territory, and data governance is, of necessity, less intense and intrusive than in more business-critical environments. Data scientists must be able to "play" with the data as, when, and how they need to—in essence, in a sandbox.

However, there soon arises an urgent and growing need to operationalize results, to feed them back and forward between the sandbox(es) and the operational environment. At this moment, of course, data governance and data (and model) management concerns become central, and—as in the case of DLC migration—the idea of a data lakehouse comes to the fore once more. And, of course, this is a valid approach. However, the relative size and value of these different modes—exploratory and operational analytics—will determine whether the data lakehouse ADP is indeed the likely preferred to-be state or if a better-managed and governed DLC pattern is a better fit in the circumstances.

Furthermore, as described in *"Catching the data mess in a data mesh"* and addressed in the data mesh ADP, we should keep in mind issues arising from the inherently distributed nature of this cloud environment and the dangers of pursuing a centralized solution. If the cross-over data requirements between the analytic and operational environments are limited, the lakehouse (or DWC/cn) ADP—despite its centralized nature—will likely suffice. Otherwise, the data mesh approach described next might be considered.

Expanding on existing operational apps in the cloud

Cloud-native businesses have, of course, always used cloud-based operational apps to run their businesses. Increasingly, the same approach is being taken by "clicks-and-mortar" businesses as many common business functions have migrated to cloud-based, Software-as-a-Service (SaaS) systems, such as Salesforce, ServiceNow, Microsoft Dynamics 365, and many more.

Such systems are built with modern software development approaches, such as microservices, DevOps, serverless, and other approaches to increase flexibility and modularity. However, their approach to providing reporting and BI function is often strongly reminiscent of prior generations of operational systems: siloed reporting and querying within the business scope of their own system and the provision of feeds or extracts to allow cross-system decision-making support. In short, they remain strongly siloed from a data warehousing perspective, and exactly the same issues that drove the evolution of data warehousing on-premises have condensed again in the cloud; but, worse, given the highly distributed and diverse nature of the cloud.

It was to mitigate these problems that data mesh was proposed (Dehghani, 2019), as described in *"Catching the data mess in a data mesh."* The conclusion, therefore, is that the data mesh ADP could be considered as a preferred destination for those upgrading existing app-centric cloud environments to support a broader and more comprehensive cloud data warehousing and analytics strategy. And there are significant numbers of supporters of this approach to be found on the web.

However, a review of such material shows (as of this writing) that the authors are typically experienced and highly skilled software engineers. Furthermore, there appears to be numerous and sometimes conflicting opinions on how to implement data mesh solutions. Software vendors have also adopted disparate positioning and offer often immature products. This demands significant, bespoke software development to deliver data mesh solutions.

We return to these questions in Volume II, where we will get ourselves more deeply entangled in data mesh. Spoiler alert: It may not be as straightforward to disentangle yourself as you might imagine.

TAKEAWAYS

- An architectural design pattern (ADP) is a set of terminology and, often, a picture, that encapsulates the key business needs and basic infrastructure requirements and constraints of a solution approach.

  Common ADPs include the three traditional patterns: data warehouse classic (DWC) both on-premises (DWC/op) and cloud-native (DWC/cn), logical data warehouse (LDW), and data lake classic (DLC).

  In addition, there exist the three modern patterns: data lakehouse and data fabric—evolutions of the DWC and LDW ADPs respectively—and data mesh—a completely novel approach.

- Most cloud data warehousing implementation journeys begin from one of three existing states, the first two of which are described by architectural design patterns:
  1. An existing DWC/op
  2. An existing DLC
  3. Ongoing cloud uptake

- A staged cloud data warehousing implementation program consists of an integrated and rolling set of projects that deliver cloud-based function and on-premises retirement. This is agreed in a staged implementation roadmap (SIR) as the basis for the journey from a DWC/op to a DWC/cn or data lakehouse ADP.

- A key consideration in moving to a DWC/cn or data lakehouse is to understand that a database built on object storage may have significantly different characteristics than traditional relational databases. These may seriously impact the migration of both queries and data preparation function.

- In many instances, the move away from a data lake approach may have already begun for data quality or even political reasons. The target state may be described as a data lakehouse or a DWC/cn, although there is little difference between the two in terms of technology. The staged implementation approach and accompanying SIR mentioned above are also applicable in this case.

- On the third journey—from an already cloud-based environment—we must consider the nature of the existing system. If it is strongly focused on analytics and AI needs, the journey is likely to echo that from the DLC pattern and the destination may be a data lakehouse or DWC/cn. Similar considerations apply in either case.

If the starting point is a cloud environment consisting of operational apps (and possibly discrete, app-centric BI and reporting tools), the data mesh ADP potentially becomes a target environment. However, this raises significant concerns about the maturity of software and methods that can support it.

- In Volume II, a more in-depth review of the target ADPs—DWC/cn, data lakehouse, data fabric, and data mesh—will explore the pros and cons of these different journeys.

Chapter 7

AND THAT'S A WRAP

I've looked at clouds from both sides now
From up and down, and still somehow
It's cloud illusions I recall
I really don't know clouds at all.

Both Sides Now, Joni Mitchell

We have indeed looked at cloud from both sides now throughout this book but, hopefully, we have a clearer understanding than the soulful, sixties' artist.

The purpose of an IT architecture is to design a structure and solution set based on available and anticipated—in the near-to medium-term—technology that addresses the known and expected needs of its projected users. The success of an architecture is thus measured, at least in part, by how long it continues to form a valid basis for application and infrastructure design. While no architecture can be expected to endure without change, the extent of change needed over time gives a further indication of its value. On the other hand, a further characteristic of a "good" architecture is in its ability to adapt to and accommodate change in both the business and technology spheres. And, not least, to assist architects and implementers to easily make good design decisions, based on what is perceived as good, reliable business and technical information.

Data warehousing, therefore, with its near four-decade history and adaptability, may be considered to be a successful architecture. In broad terms, two major iterations within this architecture can be discerned.

DATA WAREHOUSING—FIRST TIME AROUND

The first iteration, introduced in the mid-1980s and described in *"Data Warehousing: A Short History,"* can be characterized as essentially focused on delivering a single version of the truth (SVOT) via a relational-only approach. Within this model, we saw several variations as issues emerged first around development complexity and project delivery speed, and later as the business demanded ever more timely data. These variations included the hub-and-spoke approach, with a largely normalized EDW and data marts associated with Bill Inmon; the star-schema, conformed dimensional approach promoted by Ralph Kimball; and the logical data warehouse, first described by Mark Beyer of Gartner.

Such "traditional" data warehousing was the dominant model until big data became the foremost concern of the IT industry around the mid-2000s. By 2010, the big-data tsunami was seriously disrupting the relational and SVOT foundations of traditional data warehousing. Based on the idea of schema-on-read data, stored in its raw form immediately on arrival, and in a variety of NoSQL stores, the data lake paradigm emerged. Given its loose definition, it is perhaps best seen as a transitional form rather than a true architecture. However, what it showed clearly was that a relational-only technology approach was no longer viable and that a single version of the truth was increasingly incompatible with a complex digital world. In short, one size does not fit all.

CLOUD DATA WAREHOUSING—SECOND CHANCE

The second iteration of data warehousing architecture, appearing first in the early- to mid-2010s, was outlined at a conceptual level in *"Data Warehousing—Purpose and Principles"* and at a logical level in *"Cloud Data Warehousing Logical Architecture."* It continues to mature via several conflicting patterns—data lakehouse, fabric, and mesh—although it has no single, accepted name in the industry. For now, we call it *modern*, recognizing that modernity is a fleeting and ever-changeable concept. This modern data warehousing architecture is characterized by its adherence to six key considerations:

1. All data/information used by the business—ranging from operational to informational to external—may, and often will, contribute to analytics, decision making, and action taking. This full breadth must be included in the scope of the architecture. Modern data warehousing thus extends far beyond the scope of the traditional decision support and reporting needs of the business.

2. Rather than a single version of the truth, multiple but interrelated versions of truth exist in a business and, indeed, in the world at large. Whether they are in alignment or in conflict, stand-alone or closely interrelated, these many versions must be justifiable and traceable back to the underlying sources, meanings, and uses of the data and/or information on which they are based.

3. Conversely, multiple sources of truth or multiple copies of the same data/information should be avoided as far as possible to limit exponentially growing data management costs and quality issues.

4. Although a relational-only approach is no longer viable, relational database technology continues to play a key role in ensuring consistency in data/information where that is vital to running and managing the business, and in delivering information meaningfully and in a timely manner to businesspeople.

5. Context-setting information, CSI (or metadata in the broadest conceivable sense of the term) is central to the processes of defining, managing, and delivering reliable and consistent information to the business. Ontologies and knowledge graphs are increasingly key to this goal and, together with AI, play a vital role in automating these processes.

6. The delivery environment for modern data warehousing is diverse and distributed and will remain so. Hybrid on-premises and multicloud solutions are the current and future norm, and cloud-centric approaches and technologies are key to the evolution of data warehousing.

Conceptual architecture

These considerations lead directly to the conceptual architecture described in *"Three thinking spaces for cloud data warehousing."* These thinking spaces remain the same irrespective of the eventual physical location of the solution, whether on-premises or cloud. These spaces simply provide a model—people, process, and information—and the basic concepts for initial and ongoing conversations between the business and IT on what the business needs and what opportunities technology offers, as well as any limitations it imposes. Of particular concern will be the confines set by past and current technology choices as seen in *"The Journey to Cloud Data Warehousing."*

Logical information architecture

Of more interest to IT, of course, are the outcomes of these discussions and what they imply for the logical architecture. At this level, we are considering the features and functions required for data/information storage, management, and use. Here, the choice of implementation environment does have an impact on the architecture, although it turns out that the pivot from on-premises to cloud is less significant than might be expected.

The data and information domains of the tri-domain+ model remain the same. However, the information pillar structure needs to reflect the new possibilities that cloud object stores offer to consolidate data/information of different types into a common storage infrastructure. This leads to a melding of the pillars at their base, seen in its clearest form in the data lakehouse ADP. In addition, the concept of information planes is introduced into the architecture to represent the fact that data/information may reside in multiple cloud and on-premises locations.

The importance of CSI, context-setting information, has grown considerably as data/information has become ever more diverse, voluminous, and mutable, and as cloud implementations have become more widespread. At the level shown in the overall logical architecture, the depiction of CSI doesn't change due to cloud implementation. However, delving further into the needs described in cloud data ware-housing and the functionality required, CSI demands deeper thought at the technology level. This is seen in novel ap-proaches to storage structures and distributed management, as will be discussed in Volume II, particularly in the context of the data fabric ADP.

Logical process architecture

The data warehousing process architecture, as defined in 2013, doesn't need any change to accommodate novel cloud considerations. The functions defined then are still adequate to meet the needs of cloud data warehousing.

At a detailed level, the current industry focus on "pipelines" to deliver data from its sources to various targets, whether other data stores / databases or user apps, is a cause for concern. The concept of a pipeline seems to imply a sepa-rate, distinct, and "enclosed" pathway from source to target. Indeed, the way the term is used in vendor literature often reflects and encourages this thought.

However, such siloed thinking about data warehouse popu-lation directly contradicts the long-standing belief that the population process should be well-integrated and -gov-erned. This enables easier development and maintenance of the system, encourages re-use of common function, and supports the inevitable personnel change over its extended lifetime. These beliefs arise from the lessons of the "spaghetti" code environments that developed prior to and in the early days of data warehousing. Such considerations remain valid today and must be incorporated into pipeline thinking.

BLUE SKIES DATA WAREHOUSING

We approach the future of cloud data warehousing on two levels. The first level, in the conceptual architecture, leads to consideration of the pervasive and potentially pernicious spread of artificial intelligence in the people thinking space. AI simply cannot be avoided. Data warehousing implementers should carefully consider the implications of AI through ethical and societal lenses, especially where the proposed system impacts the financial and/or civil situation of users, either internal or external to the organization.

At a logical level, two areas of likely evolution are identified. First are the underpinning data storage and database considerations. Object stores will likely become the primary storage mechanism in cloud data warehousing, requiring significant enhancement to or extension of the underlying technology to cater for the record-level inserts, updates, and deletes required for streaming and other non-batched data population and preparation needs. Second is the entire area of support needed for CSI—its collection, storage, management, and use—in the highly distributed and diverse cloud data warehousing environment.

IT'S GOING TO BE SOME JOURNEY

The path to cloud data warehousing is not singular. It depends strongly on your starting point. We identify three contrasting starting points: (i) a working and successful on-premises data warehouse, (ii) a data lake, either on-premises or already in the cloud, and (iii) an existing, extensive cloud environment, focused either on analytics or on operational apps.

In the first case, the traditional precepts of staged implementation typically recommended for on-premises implementation can and should be employed. Special consideration should be given to the development of a highly distributed and diverse environment as envisaged in the data fabric ADP. In a move from a data lake, the data lakehouse ADP is likely to prove an attractive target and should also be approached via a staged implementation. Those starting with extensive cloud skills in the third case may well be attracted to data mesh thinking. However, the "bleeding edge" nature of many aspects of this approach suggests that substantial in-house development skills and experience of domain-driven design and governance will be required. Similar software maturity concerns apply to data fabric, but to a lesser extent.

AND FINALLY...

We're not finished. Not nearly.

The historical and architectural considerations we've explored here are just the beginning. No more cloud illusions, hopefully.

Understanding the near forty-year history and architecture of traditional data warehousing provides firm, reliable foundations for a successful journey to the cloud. Implementing a high-quality cloud data warehousing solution is, of course, the goal. Your journey has just begun.

Volume II is the next stage of this journey. See you there.

References

Armbrust, M., Gowda, B., Tavakoli-Shiraji, A., Xin, R., Zaharia, M., and Ghodsi, A., "Frequently Asked Questions About the Data Lakehouse", 2021, www.databricks.com/blog/2021/08/30/ frequently-asked-questions-about-the-data-lakehouse.html [accessed 2 February 2023]

Beyer, M. and Adrian, M., "Mark Beyer, Father of the Logical Data Warehouse", 2011, Gartner Blog Network, blogs.gartner.com/ merv-adrian/2011/11/03/mark-beyer-father-of-the-logical-data-warehouse-guest-post/ [accessed 1 February 2023]

Breslin, M., "Data Warehousing Battle of the Giants: Comparing the Basics of the Kimball and Inmon Models", 2004, Business Intelligence Journal, Winter 2004

Broussard, M., *Artificial Unintelligence: How Computers Misunderstand the World*, 2018, MIT Press, MA, mitpress.mit.edu/ books/artificial-unintelligence [accessed 17 March 2023]

Chamberlin, D. D. and Boyce, R. F. "SEQUEL: A structured English query language", 1974, Proc. ACM SIGMOD Workshop on Data Description, Access and Control, pp. 249-264 doi.org/10.1145/800296.811515 [accessed 9 March 2023]

Chamberlin, D. D., "Early History of SQL", 2012, IEEE Annals of the History of Computing, 34(4), ieeexplore.ieee.org/document/ 6359709 [accessed 9 March 2023]

Chen, P. P., "The Entity-Relationship Model: Toward a Unified View of Data", 1976, ACM Transactions on Database Systems, 1(1), citeseerx.ist.psu.edu/viewdoc/ summary?doi=10.1.1.123.1085 [accessed 18 March 2023]

Chessell, M., et al, "Designing and Operating a Data Reservoir", IBM ITSO, 2015, www.redbooks.ibm.com/ abstracts/ sg248274.html [accessed 14 February 2023]

Codd, E. F., "A Relational Model of Data for Large Shared Data Banks", 1970, Communications of the ACM, 13(6), dl.acm.org/doi/10.1145/362384.362685 and db.dobo.sk/wp-content/uploads/2015/11/Codd_1970_A_relational_model.pdf [accessed 9 March 2023]

Date, C. J., *An Introduction to Database Systems, 8th Ed.*, 2004, Pearson, London, UK, www.pearson.com/us/higher-education/ program/Date-An-Introduction-to-Database-Systems-8th-Edition/PGM274345.html [accessed 9 March 2023]

Dehghani, Z., "How to Move Beyond a Monolithic Data Lake to a Distributed Data Mesh", 2019, Thoughtworks, martinfowler.com/ articles/data-monolith-to-mesh.html [accessed 20 April 2022]

Dehghani, Z., *Data Mesh, Delivering Data-Driven Value at Scale*, 2022, O'Reilly Media, CA, www.oreilly.com/library/view/data-mesh/9781492092384/ [accessed 4 February 2023]

Devlin, B., *Data Warehouse: from Architecture to Implementation*, 1997, Addison Wesley, MA

Devlin, B., *Business unIntelligence: Insight and Innovation Beyond Analytics and Big Data*, 2013, Technics Publications, NJ, bit.ly/BunI-TP2 [accessed 14 February 2023]

Devlin, B., "From Layers to Pillars—A Logical Architecture for BI and Beyond", 2015, Business Intelligence Journal, Vol 20(2), 2015, bit.ly/3OolaYs [accessed 10 May 2023]

Devlin, B., "Thirty Years of Data Warehousing", 2018, Business Intelligence Journal, Vol 23 (1), 2018, bit.ly/2OatNnt [accessed 1 May 2023]

Devlin, B., "CortexDB Reinvents the Database – Full ThoughtPoint Series", 2019, bit.ly/2Yz4hkZ [accessed 10 March 2023]

Devlin, B.A. and Murphy, P.T., "An architecture for a business and information System", 1988, IBM Systems Journal, Vol 27(1), 1988, bit.ly/EBIS88 [accessed 14 February 2023]

Dixon, J., "Pentaho, Hadoop, and Data Lakes", 2010, Blog, bit.ly/2BHwplU [accessed 14 February 2023]

Evans, E., *Domain-Driven Design: Tackling Complexity in the Heart of Software*, 2003, Addison Wesley Professional MA, www.dddcommunity.org/book/evans_2003/ [accessed 4 February 2023]

Evernden, R., "The Information FrameWork", 1996, IBM Systems Journal, Vol 35(1), 1996, dl.acm.org/doi/10.1147/ sj.351.0037 [accessed 8 February 2023]

Feeney, K., "Graph Fundamentals — Part 1: RDF", 2019, medium.com/terminusdb/graph-fundamentals-part-1-rdf-60dcf8d0c459 [accessed 9 March 2023]

Frisendal, T., *Graph Data Modeling for NoSQL and SQL*, 2016, Technics Publications, NJ, technicspub.com/graph-data-modeling/ [accessed 18 March 2023]

Gartner IT Glossary, www.gartner.com/it-glossary/data-lake/ [accessed 14 February 2023]

Ghosh, P., "The Data Fabric: An Innovative Data Management Solution", 2019, Dataversity, www.dataversity.net/the-data-fabric-an-innovative-data-management-solution/ [accessed 7 February 2023]

Herskovitz, S., "Graph Normal Form", May 2021, RelationalAI blog, relational.ai/blog/graph-normal-form [accessed 12 April 2023]

IDMA and Devlin, B., *Approaches to Data Design, Engineering, and Development*, 2023 planned, IDMA 203 Course Textbook, Technics Publications, NJ

Inmon, B., *Data Lake Architecture: Designing the Data Lake and Avoiding the Garbage Dump*, 2016, Technics Publications, NJ, technicspub.com/data-lake-architecture/ [accessed 4 February 2023]

Inmon, B., Levins, M., and Srivastava, R., *Building the Data Lakehouse*, 2021, Technics Publications, NJ, technicspub.com/data-lakehouse/ [accessed 4 February 2023]

Inmon, B. and Srivastava, R., *The Data Lakehouse Architecture*, 2022, Technics Publications, NJ, technicspub.com/data-lakehouse-architecture/ [accessed 4 February 2023]

Inmon, W.H., *Building the Data Warehouse*, 1992, QED Information Sciences, MA

Inmon, W.H., Imhoff, C., and Battas, G., *Building the Operational Data Store*, 1996, Wiley & Sons, NY

Johnston, T., *Bitemporal Data: Theory and Practice*, 2014, Morgan Kaufmann, MA, www.elsevier.com/books/bitemporal-data/johnston/978-0-12-408067-6 [accessed 2 February 2023]

Jones, J., "AI could automate 25% of all jobs", April 2023, ZDNet, www.zdnet.com/article/ai-could-automate-25-of-all-jobs-heres-which-are-most-and-least-at-risk [accessed 19 April 2023]

Kimball, R., *The Data Warehouse Toolkit*, 1996, Wiley and Sons, NJ

Lorica, B., Armbrust, M., Xin, R., Zaharia, M., and Ghodsi, A., "What Is a Lakehouse?", 2020, www.databricks.com/blog/2020/01/30/what-is-a-data-lakehouse.html [accessed 2 February 2023]

March, J. G., *A Primer on Decision Making: How Decisions Happen*, 1994, The Free Press, NY, www.gsb.stanford.edu/faculty-research/books/primer-decision-making-how-decisions-happen [accessed 8 February 2023]

Moran, C., "ChatGPT is making up fake Guardian articles", The Guardian, April 2023, www.theguardian. com/commentisfree/

2023/apr/06/ai-chatgpt-guardian-technology-risks-fake-article [accessed 19 April 2023]

O'Keefe, K. and O Brien, D., *Data Ethics: Practical Strategies for Implementing Ethical Information Management and Governance*, 2023, Kogan Page, UK, www.koganpage.com/ product/data-ethics-9781398610279 [accessed 20 April 2023]

O'Neill, C., *Weapons of Math Destruction: How Big Data Increases Inequality and Threatens Democracy*, 2016, Crown Random House, NY, www.penguinrandomhouse.com/books/241363/weapons-of-math-destruction-by-cathy-oneil/ [accessed 8 February 2023]

Panetta, K., "Gartner Top 10 Data and Analytics Trends for 2021", Gartner, www.gartner.com/smarterwithgartner/ gartner-top-10-data-and-analytics-trends-for-2021 [accessed 7 February 2023]

Power, D. J., "A Brief History of Decision Support Systems", 2009, dssresources.com/history/dsshistory.html [accessed 1 April 2023]

Pratt, L., *Link: How Decision Intelligence Connects Data, Actions, and Outcomes for a Better World*, 2019, Emerald Publishing, UK, www.lorienpratt.com/linkthebook/ [accessed 29 April 2023]

Rönnbäck, L., et al, "Anchor Modeling", 2009, Proceedings of the 28th International Conference on Conceptual Modeling, Springer-Verlag, dl.acm.org/doi/10.1007/978-3-642-04840-1_19 [accessed 27 April 2023]

Sequeda, J., "What Does It Mean for a Data Catalog to Be Powered by a Knowledge Graph?", 2022, Datanami, www.datanami.com/2022/09/30/what-does-it-mean-for-a-data-catalog-to-be-powered-by-a-knowledge-graph/ [accessed 16 April 2023]

Siegel, D.J., *Mindsight: The New Science of Personal Transformation*, 2010, Bantam Press, drdansiegel.com/book/mindsight-the-new-science-of-personal-information/ [accessed 23 April 2023]

Shevlin, D., "See Beyond the 'New Normal' to the Future Reimagined: People, Process, Technology and Data", 2021, Britannic blog, www.btlnet.co.uk/insights/blog/see-beyond-the-new-normal-to-the-future-reimagined-people-process-technology-and-data [accessed 24 April 2023]

Simon, B., "Everything You Need to Know about the People, Process, Technology Framework", 2021, Smartsheet, www.smartsheet.com/content/people-process-technology [accessed 24 April 2023]

Sowa, J.F. and Zachman, J.A., "Extending and formalizing the framework for information systems architecture", 1992, IBM Systems Journal, 31(3), www.zachman.com/resources/ ea-articles-reference/50-1992-ibm-systems-journal-extending-and-formalizing-the-framework-for-information-systems-architecture [accessed 4 February 2023]

Stonebraker, M., "Why the 'Data Lake' is Really a 'Data Swamp'", 2014, Communications of the ACM, cacm.acm.org/blogs/blog-cacm/181547-why-the-data-lake-is-really-a-data-swamp/fulltext [accessed 4 February 2023]

Tiwari, N., "Unlocking the Power of Cloud-Native Technologies: The LIFESPAR Principles for Designing Resilient and Efficient Applications", 2023, LinkedIn, www.linkedin.com/pulse/unlocking-power-cloud-native-technologies-lifespar-nischal-tiwari-/ [accessed 21 April 2023]

White, A. and Heudecker, N., "The Data Lake Fallacy: All Water and Little Substance", 2014, Gartner Research, www.gartner.com/en/documents/2805917 [accessed 4 February 2023]

Yuhanna, N., "The Forrester Wave™: Enterprise Data Fabric, Q2 2020", www.forrester.com/report/the-forrester-wave-enterprise-data-fabric-q2-2020/RES157288 [accessed 7 February 2023]

Zachman, J.A., "A framework for information systems architecture", 1987, IBM Systems Journal, 26(3), 1987 www.zachman.com/resource/ea-articles/49-1987-ibm-systems-journal-a-framework-for-information-systems-architecture [accessed 8 February 2023]

INDEX

Page numbers in **bold** indicate definitions.

3 Vs 36

analytical applications 180

analytics **12**, 37, 182

Analytics and Business
Intelligence (ABI) 13

Apache Hudi 144

Apache Iceberg 144

Apache Spark 39, 165

architectural design pattern
(ADP) **162**

artificial intelligence (AI) 4, 136,
196

augmentation 139

automation 137

generative 139

big bang project 168

big data 37, 191

Big Data Ocean 49

bulk capture **118**

business data directory 14

business data warehouse 14

business domain 44

business intelligence (BI) 3, 180

CapEx vs. OpEx 180

centralization 65

change data capture **119**

cleansing **122**

clickstream 31

cloud data warehousing **4**

modern principles 68

cloud-native 164

conceptual architecture **74**, 193

consistency vs. timeliness 175

context, creation and usage 59,
153

context-setting info. (CSI) 69,
100, 123, 125, 150, 193, 194

data

cleansing 24

consistency 23

exhaust 52

integration 65

layering 20, 65, 107

meaning 23

naked **61**, 153

raw 41, 81

real-time 124

semi-structured 81

silo 108
timeliness 23, 24
data as a product 45, 166
data dictionary 14
data engineering 48
data fabric **27**, 114, 132, 151, 166
data federation 125
data governance &
management 46, 49, 71, 125,
177, 181, 183
automation 153
data lake 19, 31, 51, 191
data lake classic (DLC) **165**, 174
data lakehouse 31, **39**, 114, 144,
165, 176, 179, 183, 194, 197
data mart 19, 20
data mesh **43**, 132, 151, 166, 183,
184, 185
data modeling 130, 152
data pipeline **127**
data processing 61
data quality 24, 51, 65, 66, 96,
109, 125, 167, 175
data reservoir 33
data science 183
data swamp 35, 175
data virtualization 125, 165
data vs. information 57
data warehouse 16
dimensional 21
federated 25
star-schema 21

virtual 25
data warehouse classic (DWC)
163
data warehousing **3**
modern principles 68
purpose 56
data wrangling 120, 154
database administration 182
decision intelligence **143**
decision-making support **12**
declarative vs. procedural 36
derivation **121**
DevOps 184
Digital Information Systems
Architecture (DISA) 6, 75
dimension, conformed 22
direct access **119**
distributed data architecture 45
domain-driven design 44, 166
drill-down 21
EMEA Business Information
System (EBIS) 13, 25
enterprise data model (EDM) 17,
66, 69
enterprise data warehouse
(EDW) 20, 24, 46, 48, 66, 190
entity-relationship (ER)
modeling 152
ethics 139, 196
event **105**
externally sourced data 178

extract, load, and transform
(ELT)   173
extract, transform, and load
(ETL)   16, 48, **119**, 123, 126
fact   57
garbage in, garbage out   24
graph database   146
graph normal form (GNF)   155
Hadoop   36, 167
hub-and-spoke   190
human-sourced information
(HSI)   94, **99**
hybrid on-premises/cloud   181,
193
IDEAL   76
immediate capture   **118**
information   **58**
   multiplex   81
   pillars   92, **104**
   pillars, partitioning   108
   planes   **112**
   unstructured   81
information context
   management system   154
information modeling   152
information preparation 116, 178
information thinking space   68,
78, 93
   reliance/usage   82, 111
   timeliness/consistency   80
informational systems   16, 64

innovation   67
integrated   18
internet of things (IoT)   31, 93,
98, 144
Island of Information   49, 176
knowledge   149
knowledge graph   **150**, 193
   connected   28
labeled property graph (LPG)
   146
Lake of Data   49, 176
Land of the Enterprise   48
LIFESPAR   173
lift-and-shift   164, 174
logical architecture   92, 93, 194
   administration   **130**
   assimilation   **121**, 125
   choreography   **132**
   instantiation   **117**
   reification   **124**
   utilization   **128**
logical data warehouse (LDW)
   26, **164**, 190
machine learning   151
machine-generated data (MGD)
   94, **97**, 144
mappa mundi   48
master data management
   (MDM)   66
meaning   150
   implicit/tacit   82

measure   **105**

message   **105**

metadata   29, 35, 69, 193

   active   28, 166

   business   149

microservices   132, 184

model management   183

multicloud   **113**, 181, 193

nonvolatile   17

NoSQL   26, 191

object store   144, 172, 196

on-premises 93, 97, 104, 112, 113,
   163

ontology   148, 193

operational BI   23

operational data store (ODS) 23

operational systems   16, 64

people thinking space   72, **86**,
   138

    information intent   87

    organizational role   86

    psychosocial mindset   88

pipeline   45, 195

process thinking space   71, **83**

   active scope   83

   business effect   84

   time span   85

process-mediated data (PMD)
       31, 37, 94, **96**, 144

program-based project
   management   20

rational decision theory   88

REAL   **115**

reconciliation   81, **122**

relational database (RDB) 20, 25,
   146

replication   119

reporting   180

resource description framework
   (RDF)   **147**

schema-on-read   32, 176, 191

schema-on-write   179

semantic inconsistency   **122**

semantic layer   26, 151

semantic model   46

serverless   184

service delivery agreement   110

service oriented architecture
   (SOA)   84

service-oriented architecture
   (SOA)   132

services catalogue   130

silos   184

single version of the truth
   (SVOT)   18, 190, 192

sixth normal form (6NF)   155

slice-and-dice   21

social media   93

software engineering   48, 72

Software-as-a-Service (SaaS) 184

SQL   142, 146

staged implementation   197

staged implementation
   roadmap (SIR)   169

streaming 118

subject-oriented 17

technochauvinism 141

temporal inconsistency **122**

thinking space **75**, 193

timestamp 18

time-variant 18

transaction **106**

transaction generation **120**

tri-domain+ model **94**, 194

triple store 147

www.ingramcontent.com/pod-product-compliance
Lightning Source LLC
Chambersburg PA
CBHW071242050326
40690CB00011B/2233